GOETHE
A Critical Introduction

GOETHE

A Critical Introduction

By Henry Hatfield

Harvard University Press
Cambridge, Massachusetts
1964

© 1963 by Henry Hatfield
Library of Congress Catalog Card Number 64-24031

Published by arrangement with New Directions.

The selections from the *Faust* translation of Louis MacNeice, Copyright 1951 by Louis MacNeice. The selections from the *Faust, Part I* translation of C. F. MacIntyre, Copyright 1949 by New Directions.

Manufactured in the United States of America.

For
PETER GAY AND JACK STEIN

FOREWORD TO THE HARVARD EDITION

This book is virtually identical with its paperback edition (New Directions, 1963). Two or three typographical errors have been corrected, and a very few further minor alterations have been made.

I am most grateful to James Laughlin and Robert MacGregor of New Directions, and equally so to the Syndics and staff of the Harvard University Press, for their cooperation in the present venture. Appearing in two different formats, the book may perhaps reach a more varied audience than would otherwise be the case. For helpful criticism and appreciation I must thank many friends, especially Alexander Gerschenkron, Winfred Lehmann, Harry Levin, Joan Neider, and William W. Pusey III.

Henry Hatfield

Cambridge, Massachusetts
May, 1964

PREFACE

GOETHE IS A "MAKER OF MODERN LITERATURE" IN MORE ways than one, not least through the impact of his work and personality on writers from Ibsen to Mann and Gide. If some of his writings have receded into the "coulisses of time," others were not seen in their real importance until the twentieth century: works like *The Elective Affinities*, the poems of his lyrical cycle the *Divan*, the second part of *Faust*. His finest work is modern and much more: it has become part of the timeless, simultaneous order of literature which T. S. Eliot has defined. In a sense which has nothing to do with literary labels, it is classic, a "possession forever." Often Goethe's poetry recalls his own aphorism: "Everything perfect in its own kind must transcend its kind; it must become something different and incomparable."

This book is intended mainly as a guide, with "program notes," to Goethe's works. It could not pretend to treat all of them; I have concentrated on those writings of his which seem to me the most vital and fresh. Of course many of his lyrics are included. As an introduction, the book does not take any previous knowledge of Goethe or of the German language for granted. I do not claim to say anything radically new about the poet but hope that those who already know him well may be interested in some of the book's emphases and nuances.

Essentially this book consists of interpretations of Goethe's works, complemented by a reasonable minimum of biography and "background material." The arrangement is roughly chronological, except that it seemed convenient to treat the first part of *Faust* together with the second part, Goethe's last great achievement. While trying to focus on the text, I have not excluded Goethe's own statements about his aims. Rather, while I have of course aimed to keep the given work of art at the center of attention, I have also drawn on what has been said about it, by the author or anyone else, as seemed sensible in each instance. By now it is a truism that a writer may be deceived about his own intentions; but to assume that his comments should therefore be disregarded would be something else again. In dealing with a writer of Goethe's tremendous intelligence, it would be downright silly. While some of the thousands of his remarks about his various writings contradict each other—they were recorded over a span of some sixty years—they form, taken as a whole, a surprisingly objective interpretation, not infallible of course, but indispensable.

I am much indebted to various standard German books about Goethe and editions of his works, especially to those edited by Trunz and Ernst Beutler, and to Wilhelm

PREFACE

Emrich's interpretation of *Faust II*. Also I owe a great deal to Santayana's *Three Philosophical Poets*, Miss E. M. Wilkinson's essays on *Tasso*, and the *Faust* commentaries of Stuart Atkins and Alexander Gillies; and above all to the books and lectures of Barker Fairley, which fuse close knowledge of Goethe, literary flair and verve, and a felicitous style in the happiest of combinations. My specific debts to these and other scholars are recorded in the Notes.

It is almost impossible to find adequate translations of Goethe's poetry. For the lyrics I have generally made prose translations. For *Faust*, a combination of MacIntyre, MacNeice, Bayard Taylor, and one or two others has been used; here the original meters have been preserved. (Translations not listed under "Acknowledgments"—p. 233—are my own.)

Particularly I must thank Peter Gay, James Laughlin, Robert MacGregor, and Robert Spaethling for careful readings of the manuscript, and Jane Hatfield for many helpful suggestions and for devoting much of her "vacation" to typing it. I am also grateful to the staffs of the Baker Library of Dartmouth College and of Widener Library for their courteous assistance.

H. H.

Cambridge, Mass.
October, 1962

CONTENTS

1. INTRODUCTION. Profile of Goethe's achievement. The German literary and political situation in the eighteenth century. 1
2. STORM AND STRESS. Frankfurt. Early writings. Herder. Goethe's first characteristic works. *Götz von Berlichingen.* Storm and Stress Odes. *Werther.* 19
3. RESOLUTION AND FIRST MATURITY. The turn toward "objective" verse. *Egmont.* Weimar. *Wilhelm Meister's Theatrical Mission. Iphigenia. Tasso.* Lyrics. 42
4. TOWARD A NEW CLASSICISM. Italy. *Roman Elegies* and *Venetian Epigrams.* Impact of the French Revolution. *Wilhelm Meister's Apprenticeship.* "Classical" lyrics. *Hermann and Dorothea.* 73
5. IRONY AND RENUNCIATION. Political and literary developments. *The Elective Affinities. Pandora. Poetry and Truth. Divan. Wilhelm Meister's Wanderjahre.* Late poems. 99
6. FAUST I: The Little World 132
7. FAUST II: The Great World 177
   NOTES 223
   A BRIEF LIST OF WORKS IN ENGLISH 229
   ACKNOWLEDGMENTS 233
   INDEX 235

1. INTRODUCTION

1. Johann Wolfgang von Goethe: A Profile

WHEN DEALING WITH WRITERS OF THE HIGHEST RANK, THE proper question, as Emil Staiger has suggested, is not: "What do we think of Goethe (or Shakespeare, or Plato)?" but "What would Goethe have thought of us?" In America, at least, he is more often mentioned approvingly than read, and many have at best a more or less distinct impression of the action of *Faust*. It thus seems appropriate to sum up his career in a few pages and then to sketch in the literary background, before turning to his most significant works.

Goethe's long life (1749–1832) coincided with the most exciting and creative period since the Renaissance: he was more or less contemporary with the heroes of the French Revolution and of the Napoleonic Wars; with Kant and Hegel, Mozart and Beethoven; with Schiller and the whole galaxy of romantic poets from Blake to Brentano. Indeed, what is sometimes called the Age of Goethe may well be viewed as the German form of the

Renaissance, the belated flowering of German literature and thought. His work forms a great arch connecting the eighteenth and nineteenth centuries, a still feudal Rococo society with the Industrial Revolution. One of the dominant figures of European romanticism, he was at the same time a keen critic of the romantic mind. At times he reminds us of Racine or Voltaire, at others of Byron or Wordsworth. As Thomas Mann put it, he united the vigor of Luther with the urbanity of Erasmus.

Among the writers generally considered supremely great, Goethe has one very practical attraction from the reader's point of view: he is closest to us in time, and hence in some ways the most accessible. To read Dante with some degree of comprehension, for example, one has to have a certain grasp of medieval thought; Greek tragedy presents us with a view of the divine powers and of human responsibility to which we must consciously adjust ourselves. Goethe, on the other hand, reacted to forces which still affect us directly today: the impact of the ideas of the French Revolution, the rise of industry and collectivism, the tension between an other-worldly and a "this-worldly" view of life.

Yet, since about the time of the First World War, Goethe's reputation has been to some degree eclipsed in England and the United States; he has been attacked by a few influential critics and ignored by more. T. S. Eliot's early verdict—since withdrawn—was that Goethe "dabbled in both philosophy and poetry and made no great success of either." (Eliot reversed himself very gracefully later: he now ranks Goethe with Shakespeare and Dante as one of the three representative European poets.) By

INTRODUCTION

quoting Faust's words "Feeling is all" completely out of context, Irving Babbitt made Goethe appear an archromantic, and exposed him to the scorn of all right-thinking New Humanists. (Obviously, to ascribe to the author the views of one of his dramatic heroes is not cricket.) Unfair though Babbitt's interpretation was, it had a considerable effect. But there were broader reasons for the anti-Goethean mood of the Twenties and Thirties: Goethe seemed remote from the harsh problems of the time; he was suspect as the hero of Victorian idealism; he was in some sense a romantic; the professorial image of a plaster-cast Olympian Goethe in fact deserved to be smashed; and finally, it was all too natural to regard anything German skeptically. Read in translation, and without the "corrective" of the Second Part, *Faust I* does seem only the "near masterpiece" a critic called it in 1932 in an essay significantly entitled "What Is Left of Goethe?" While there is something irritating about this title, naive arrogance is perhaps better than perfunctory praise.

While Goethe's general prestige in English-speaking countries diminished in the twentieth century, his impact on literature continued to be great. For an older generation, he had been linked with Ibsen and Browning as a culture hero. Perhaps the loss of this particular type of glory was no real deprivation. At any rate, Goethe's appeal to writers of the first rank has remained great. Neither *The Magic Mountain*, the *Joseph* novels, nor much of Gide, nor of course Valéry's *Mon Faust*, nor the "Walpurgis Night" sections in *Ulysses* could have been written without his example. On a lower but still very decent level, books like Hermann Hesse's *Steppenwolf* and *Magister Ludi* and Hofmannsthal's *Death and the Fool* show a similar indebtedness.

The sheer bulk of Goethe's achievements is almost frightening—and I am referring only to achievements of the first order. Clearly, he is the most uneven of great writers, and much that is included in the 143 volumes of the standard "Weimar edition" falls short. No one would urge that *The Fellow Culprits, Clavigo,* or *The Citizen General* is an important drama; nor, obviously, are all the thousands of lyrics and pages of prose on the level of his finest work. Surely, however, a writer deserves to be judged by his best. "Where one cannot love, one should pass by," Goethe himself remarked. This advice will be taken here: I intend to concentrate in this book on Goethe's clear successes, on works still fresh, pertinent, and "splendid like the primal day."

It is first of all as a lyric poet that we think of Goethe; no other has his scope. At times his lyrics recall Sappho's, at times the folk song; in Rome, he wrote—successfully—in the mode of Tibullus and Propertius. He ranged from the simple songs of his Strasbourg days through the defiant hymns of his "Storm and Stress" era to elaborate reworkings of classic, Italian, and Oriental forms; from deliberately artificial Rococo trifles to profound philosophical poems like "Holy Longing" and "Testament" ("Vermächtnis"). In the poetry of his old age, especially in the *Divan*, he often appears as a master of irony, writing behind a mask as it were, in a tone simultaneously serious and light. His arsenal of metrical forms is equally inclusive: he seems as much at home in simple four-line stanzas as in the sonnet, in *ottava rima* and the distich

INTRODUCTION

as in free verse. There is one important exception: he avoided such pre-eminently classical patterns as the Sapphic and the Alcaic, although they had been used with striking success by his predecessor Klopstock. Apparently he felt that they were nevertheless alien to the spirit and tradition of German verse.

The lyrical impulse in Goethe—the pouring forth of the individual emotion felt here and now—is manifest in his novels and dramas as well. I am not referring to the songs inserted in prose works—magnificent as the "Mignon" lyrics in *Wilhelm Meister's Apprenticeship* are —but to a certain crypto-lyricism. Thus many of Werther's letters are poems in prose; in *Tasso*, we hear and see the poet-protagonist composing before us. This drama is written entirely in lovely, smoothly flowing blank verse; when Tasso launches himself into one of his imaginative flights, we have poetry raised to the second power. Often in *Faust*, especially in the First Part, the characters do not so much converse as say their pieces, sing their songs. They "speak past one another," as the German expression has it.

In the drama, Goethe is equally versatile though not of equal greatness. We can safely ignore his youthful Rococo works, set in Alexandrines; and the "occasional plays" written for the Weimar court have little to recommend them besides a few lovely inserted lyrics. Some of his boisterous youthful farces, however, have been unjustly neglected. Of the major plays, it is perhaps the more or less Shakespearean ones, *Götz von Berlichingen* and *Egmont*—the latter owing much to *Julius Caesar*— which have aged the most.

At the opposite pole are the dramas of interior action, *Iphigenia in Tauris, Torquato Tasso,* and, at some remove, *The Natural Daughter.* Owing much to Racine, these plays observe the neo-classic unities, carry courtly decorum almost to an extreme, and are set in a regular blank verse which attains a melodiousness hardly reached before in German poetry. What action they contain is largely symbolic: in both *Iphigenia* and *Tasso* swords are drawn at moments of tension, but no duel is fought. In both plays, symmetrically arranged pairs of characters—Iphigenia and Orestes, Tasso and Antonio, and so on—illustrate the balance which is the mark of Goethe's early classicism. While neither is dramatic in an obvious sense, both have a subtle power as well as great psychological penetration; they are by no means mere "closet dramas."

Towering above the other plays stands the unique dramatic poem *Faust.* The product of some sixty years of intermittent effort, *Faust* naturally has its inconsistencies, formal imperfections, and unresolved problems. We are not even sure of just what Goethe meant when he called it a tragedy—though a hypothetical solution will be suggested later in this book. One point is clear: the long poem has challenged the mind and imagination of modern man as few other works of literature have done. Like Hamlet, Don Giovanni, and Don Quixote, Faust is one of the rare figures who have become genuinely mythical. If a great deal of bombast has been written about "Faustian man," that is one of the tributes which mediocrity exacts from greatness. Without Faust, we should scarcely have had Peer Gynt, Captain Ahab, or Nietzsche's Zarathustra—the last a dubious boon, to be sure. It should

INTRODUCTION

be added that *Faust* is eminently stageable. Even the Second Part, which was not properly appreciated until the twentieth century, is extremely effective drama when tactfully cut and played *con brio*. To see it acted by a first-rate cast is a genuine theatrical experience.

Goethe's first novel, *The Sorrows of Young Werther* (1774), was also his first international success; its vogue seems to have influenced mores as well as habits of dress and letter-writing; it became in fact an embarrassment to him. While this story of the suicide of a frustrated young man is the product of a sentimental age, it transcends the time of its origin. As a tragedy of adolescence, *Werther* is not antiquated; nor is it dated as a formal work of art. Rather surprisingly, this emotionally charged novel which Goethe wrote at the highest pitch, in a few weeks, is characterized by an exquisitely balanced symmetry. It is also the classic example, though not the first, of his way of procuring emotional catharsis by composing a "confessional" work. The poet was himself involved in a triangular situation like that described in the novel. Unlike poor Werther, he could purge himself and go on to other loves—and other books. The pattern was to be repeated again and again.

Far less unified aesthetically, *Wilhelm Meister's Apprenticeship* (1795–96) is one of the most influential novels ever written. It is the archetype of the *Bildungsroman*: the novel which tells of the formation of a young man's character, mind, and tastes, generally tracing his development from early youth to a point when he has achieved a certain degree of maturity. *Wilhelm Meister* is not the first in time of its genre, but it has had by far the greatest impact. Most important German novels, from the romantic movement, through mid-nineteenth-century works like Keller's *Green Henry* and Stifter's *Indian Summer* to Mann's *The Magic Mountain* and Hesse's major books, are of this type. It is ironically varied in Kafka's *Amerika* and parodied in Mann's *Felix Krull*. In England, largely through Carlyle's translation, Wilhelm Meister's "English kinsmen" appear in Dickens, Meredith, Butler's *The Way of All Flesh*, and scores of lesser narratives. Less influential in France, the *Bildungsroman* model is still evident in the early novels of Anatole France and in Romain Rolland's *Jean Christophe*. Perhaps the relatively cool French reaction may be explained by differences in sense of form. The educational novel tends to be long, deliberate, and excursive: its unity is found mainly in the developing style of a personality emerging gradually in an extended series of experiences; there is no sharpness of focus. *Meister's Apprenticeship*, finished some twenty years after its inception, is particularly episodic, indeed inorganic. In this regard, its impact on German fiction was an unhappy one.

By definition, books in this tradition tend to be optimistic, and seriously concerned with the individual and his culture. While the *Bildungsroman,* at its most representative, is not concerned with material success, it is linked socially with the rise of the middle class to self-awareness and self-respect.

In *The Elective Affinities* (1809), Goethe returned to the tight structure of *Werther*. Here too, the halves of the novel are kept in careful balance; thematic parallels and leitmotifs hold the work together. *The Elective Affinities* is a subtle and penetrating study of the relations among four human beings; on a different level, of the clash between the natural and the moral law as exemplified by questions of marriage and divorce. The book is remarkably daring for its time; debate is still going on about its intention. Does it demonstrate the determinism implied in its title? (An elective affinity, in chemistry, denotes the irresistible mutual attraction between two elements.) Or does the novel uphold the absolute sanctity of marriage, as Goethe himself stated more than once? The question is made harder to answer by Goethe's inclination to irony, especially in his middle and later years. Lord Byron was not entirely mistaken when he called him an old fox.

Goethe's last novel, *Wilhelm Meister's Wanderjahre* (1821; revised 1829) is not a unified narrative but a broad intermingling of social and ethical reflections and novellas with the account of Wilhelm's journeys. Its subtitle, "The Renouncers," shows that it stands at the farthest remove from Faust's belief in self-fulfillment. And while *Faust*, like *Meister's Apprenticeship*, is essentially concerned with the development of the individual, the *Wanderjahre* is focused on the group and its needs. It is full of fascinating, often prophetic, insights into matters of education, of the rise of industrialism and collectivism, of the whole sweep of the nineteenth century. While there have been distinguished attempts to show that it is also a work of art, these efforts are not really convincing.

Of the host of works in other genres, only a few can be mentioned here. *Hermann and Dorothea* (1797), a poem in dactylic hexameters, is a unique fusion of Homeric epic and domestic idyll: Goethe wished to show both the heroic character of the age of the revolution—symbolized in the statuesque Dorothea—and the staunch, conservative values of small-town Germany—epitomized in the respectable if unexciting Hermann. Benedetto Croce objected to this combination of disparate strains; but actually Goethe's gently ironic use of the hexameter expresses the quasi-heroic, quasi-bourgeois theme very nicely; form mirrors content.

Shorter fiction was not one of Goethe's major strengths: the novellas of his *Entertainments of German Emigrés* (1795, modeled after the *Decameron*), like those included in the *Wanderjahre,* are competent and interesting rather than brilliant. Yet in his enigmatic "The Fairy Tale" and the equally elusive "Novella" (1795 and 1828), he wrote symbolic narratives in a hauntingly romantic vein.

Avowedly, Goethe was an opponent of satire: treat only what you love. In fact, however, there are brilliant satiric passages in *Faust* (mainly directed against professors), in the early farces, and elsewhere. *Reynard the Fox* (1794) recasts medieval tales of the clever fox in an amoral world; its tone is uncharacteristically harsh. The French Revolution shocked the poet severely; for some years, in the Nineties, his mood was predominantly negative and bitter. Goethe joined forces with Schiller to produce in the distichs of the *Xenia* (1797) a polemical survey of contemporary life and literature. The result is almost a "Ship of Fools."

In his later years, Goethe began to regard his own career historically: he could examine his life with some objectivity, even with flashes of irony. Thus his autobiography *Poetry and Truth* (1811–33), which recounts his

INTRODUCTION

life from his birth to his departure for Weimar in 1775, is not fervidly self-centered in the manner of St. Augustine or Rousseau, but paints a fresco of a quarter-century of German life, not only of his own role. Yet it is marked by a sure sense of his own destiny. At the end of *Poetry and Truth,* writing of the decision to attach himself to the ducal court at Weimar which was to affect all the rest of his life decisively, he quoted one of his own heroes, the fatalist Egmont:

> . . . As if whipped by invisible spirits, the sun-horses of Time bolt with the frail chariot of our fate, and nothing is left for us but to grasp the reins courageously and hold fast; and to guide the wheels, now to the right, now to the left, away from the rock on this side and the precipice on that. Whither we are bound, who knows? He barely remembers, after all, from where he came.

Goethe's *Italian Journey* (1816–17) is the somewhat stylized account of his attempt to find the classical ideal—to become as it were a Greek reborn—by immersing himself in the atmosphere of Rome and Sicily. For generations who no longer equate Rome with fifth-century Athens, and who cannot believe with Winckelmann that ancient life was the full realization of "noble simplicity and quiet grandeur," the *Italian Journey* has lost much if its immediacy; but it remains an impressive document, especially interesting in its revolt against Christianity in the name of an aesthetically oriented, "this-worldly" humanism.

Not the least of Goethe's gifts was his flair for literary criticism. This is especially evident in Eckermann's *Conversations with Goethe,* which Nietzsche called, with less than his usual exaggeration, the greatest book in the German language. To be sure, the Olympian Goethe, uttering solemn *pronunciamentos* to the "devout Eckermann"— as Melville called him—can be at times a little hard to take. But Eckermann, his literary assistant for many years, had an understandable tendency to "mythify" the poet, and above all, we must not let an occasional stiffness of language obscure the lithe thrust of Goethe's thought and wit. "When a book and a head collide, and there is a hollow sound, it isn't necessarily the fault of the book," Lichtenberg observed. Goethe's discussion of Byron shows him at his critical best. To the Philistine objection that the amoral British poet could not be a force for true culture (*Bildend*), he retorted: "Everything great has formative force, as soon as we perceive it," and went on to emphasize Byron's "boldness, audacity, and grandiosity." No idolater, he remarked elsewhere of Byron that "as soon as he sets up as a thinker, he becomes a child." The collection *Maxims and Reflections,* composed of aphorisms mainly written in old age, is an equally abundant source of Goethe's wisdom.

One wearies of recounting Goethe's achievements; he is simply too great for us. Possibly the decline in his fame stems largely from the natural human resentment against an Aristides who is always called the just. The account must nevertheless be continued: he was an excellent translator—even as a child, he had an almost unique flair for languages—and made admirable renderings of Cellini, Voltaire, and Diderot, among others. As if this were not enough, one must add that he was gifted in painting and drawing; until he had seen the treasures of Rome, he

INTRODUCTION

thought that art was his main talent. He directed the Weimar theater for many years, and often appeared on the stage himself as an amateur actor in his earlier time there.

Before his Italian journey (1786–88), Goethe devoted long years of self-sacrificing labor to administration, as one of the chief officials of the Duchy of Weimar. It is almost incredible that the great lyrics of his first eleven years there, as well as the first version of *Iphigenia* and long sections of other works, were written more or less in his free hours, as it were with his left hand. It is frightening to think that the greatest writer of modern times devoted himself for almost eleven years to such tasks as drafting recruits for the ducal army, managing the fire department, and rehabilitating the mining industry in a nearby town. This was no part-time job, like Kafka's position in an insurance company; no sinecure like Hawthorne's in the customs house. No doubt this altruistic labor was salutary up to a point; but inevitably the forced alienation from his own genius made him almost literally ill. Fragments of unfinished works were accumulating; some would be finished in Italy, some even later. The flight to Rome was a return to himself.

It is difficult for one who is not a scientist to write sensibly of Goethe's contributions to anatomy, botany, and so forth. We know that he was one of the discoverers of the intermaxillary bone in man; that he was at least not entirely wrong in his long quarrel with Newton about the theory of color; that, though he was not a direct precursor of Darwin, his sense of metamorphosis, of the upward sweep of all life, foreshadowed the shape of evolutionary theories to come, as the career of Homunculus, in *Faust II*, makes especially clear. Goethe's belief in the archetypal plant (*Urpflanze*), the archetypal man, horse, etc., is not evolutionary in a temporal sense: rather, he held that the pure forms of plant, man, horse, and so on, exist concretely, and that all the variants of whatever class derive from such archetypes.

This is all very impressive, but it is not Goethe's breadth of interest and talents that really matters. If he had merely been a gifted amateur or promising second-rater in all these fields, his universality would at most inspire a rather cold admiration. It is not on his versatility but on his intensity—his absolute achievement in the lyric, in *Faust*, in a few other works—that his greatness is truly founded.

2. The Literary Situation

"WHEN I WAS EIGHTEEN," GOETHE ONCE REMARKED TO Eckermann, "Germany was only eighteen itself, and there was still something to be done. . . ." Varying this observation, one could say that when Goethe was born, modern German literature was still in its cradle: the first cantos of Klopstock's *Messias* had been published only a year before, in 1748. These solemn, soaring hexameters did indeed mark the birth of a literary revolution; aside from them and Klopstock's early odes, the situation was dismal enough. A few worthy writers, the so-called Anacreontics, wrote little verses in praise of love, wine, and friendship. These part-time versifiers, who avowedly devoted only their leisure hours to the Muse, were careful to declare

INTRODUCTION

that though their verse might seem wanton, their life was chaste. German "Anacreontic" verse is a minor expression of the Rococo, far inferior to Rococo music or architecture. Liberating influences, to be sure, had been reaching Germany from England since the late seventeenth century, but their full force had not been felt. Still, in descriptive nature poetry, in the sentimentalism of Richardson (which appealed to the "inwardness" of the native Pietist tradition), and above all in the vogue of Milton, the British impact was increasing.

For the time being, however, the prestige of French literature was predominant. It was symbolic that young Frederick II ("the Great") invited Voltaire to Prussia; the concentration of *philosophes* in Potsdam, with the King and Voltaire as its two foci, has well been called "the apex of the century." It was not merely or primarily that the French were the acknowledged masters of neoclassic tragedy, of comedy, Rococo verse, and form generally. Above all, they were the exemplars and transmitters of the Enlightenment, of doubt both skeptical and creative. Voltaire's works and Bayle's *Dictionary* were smuggled into the pious seminary where the young poet Wieland was being educated; Lessing, though he disliked Voltaire, was heavily in his intellectual debt. With a few honorable exceptions, German scholars have tended often to underrate, more often to deplore, the influence of France. Goethe felt differently. As a boy, he regularly attended the French theater in Frankfurt; he often translated from the French; and in old age he declared that it was impossible for him to hate a nation to which he owed so great a part of his own culture.

While the liberating power of the Enlightenment had begun to transform education, law, and mores and had found expression in respectable poets like Albrecht von Haller, no literary genius had as yet taken the torch of the *Aufklärung* from France or England. Lessing and Wieland were still obscure. German criticism consisted largely of applying the codified rationalism of Wolff to the neoclassic tradition. Mildly liberal pre-romantic impulses were felt from Zürich, where two Swiss critics championed the rights of the imagination and the miraculous in poetry, thus arousing the anger of the conservatives. It was a very minor and provincial controversy, however: few people today read the polemics of these Gottscheds, Bodmers, and Breitingers except when forced to by graduate schools. In part, the versified enthusiasm for Frederick II may be connected with the new spirit; was not the Prussian king, to most observers, the very model of the enlightened ruler? Goethe himself testified that the deeds of Frederick first provided German poetry with an authentic, vital theme. Actually, however, it was Klopstock, no admirer of that monarch, who began the new movement: he took both poetry and himself seriously, and was a pioneer both in form and in the lofty—often all-too-lofty—expression of his emotions.

By the late 1760's, the whole atmosphere had changed. Klopstock had revolutionized the lyric; Winckelmann's evocations of Greek art and the Greek ethos had laid the foundations for the new classicism which was to arise in Weimar some twenty years later. C. M. Wieland had published his first important works, including *Agathon*, the educational novel which really established the genre in

INTRODUCTION

Germany. In his *Hamburg Dramaturgy*, Lessing attempted to replace neo-classic theory by reinstating the authentic doctrine of Aristotle. Here and elsewhere, he pointed to Shakespeare, rather than to Voltaire or Corneille, as the proper inspiration of German playwrights. He was not alone in championing Shakespeare. Of the several German critics who helped to 'rediscover' the Elizabethan, Johann Gottfried Herder was perhaps the most influential, and certainly the most helpful to Goethe. He did not maintain—as Lessing had done—that Shakespeare wrote in unconscious harmony with Aristotle's principles, but rather that he was a genius understandable only in terms of his own time, of the English milieu, and of national traditions. Along with this enthusiasm, other influences came flooding in from England. The most important were Edward Young's cult of original genius, the sentimental "Ossianic" poetry of Macpherson, the interest in the folk song as exemplified by Bishop Percy's *Reliques of Ancient English Poetry*, and the interpretation of Homer in terms of his time and native region.

If the impact of French culture was somewhat obscured by that of the British, it remained great; but its direction had somewhat changed. Rousseau had become a name to conjure with, less in political theory than in matters of education, of manners, of the heart. Without his—perhaps misunderstood—summons to return to nature, the German literary revolution would have run a different course. Werther's cult of nature and of his own soul owed much to Jean-Jacques. Diderot reinforced this "preromantic" tendency. Writing of himself and his youthful companions in Strasbourg, Goethe noted that they were chilled by the "mechanical" style of the *Encyclopédie*, but entranced by Diderot's "children of nature" and strengthened in their aversion to conventional society by his view of it. All of these writers, both French and English, contributed to the formation of Goethe's mind. At least as important as any of them was the Bible, in Luther's translation. Goethe was saturated in it from boyhood on; throughout his life, he drew on Biblical language and imagery in his letters and conversations as well as in his works.

In the eighteenth century, Germany was a collection of some 300 units large and small—kingdoms, duchies, ecclesiastical states, free "imperial cities," like Frankfurt on the Main, where the poet was born, and so on. Theoretically, all of these political entities were subject to the Holy Roman Empire, but the impotence of that ancient superstate had long been evident. The economy of "the Germanies" was mainly agricultural, their class structure feudal, their total population less than that of France. In comparison to the English middle class, the German lived a cramped existence, with little freedom or prestige; it is no wonder that sensitive intellectuals tended to introversion. However regrettable this "inwardness" may have been from the practical and psychological points of view, it fostered the growth of philosophy, music, and literature, of a new culture with some of the attributes of a secularized religion. Finally, the time was a relatively peaceful one; the various wars fought on German soil were of the limited type, unlike the total disaster of the Thirty Years War in the preceding century. Probably this partly explains the tone of optimism one senses in much of the thought and the art of the era.

2. STORM AND STRESS

GOETHE BECAME AWARE ONLY GRADUALLY OF THE FORCES which were beginning to transform German literature and thought. To be sure, his native Frankfurt was colorful and interesting, and the society of "patrician" burgher families into which he was born was a rather cultivated one. Goethe's mother was warmhearted and imaginative; he attributed the basically cheerful side of his nature to her, as well as his joy in telling tales. Only eighteen at his birth, she had a vigor and gaiety which his father Johann Kaspar Goethe (who was much older than she) sadly lacked. At the time of his marriage he had already retired from taking any part in Frankfurt affairs. While cultivated and intelligent, he seems to have been stiff and over-conscientious; a dignified but rather pathetic man who had been defeated by life.

It was an exciting time: events like the French occupation during the Seven Years War and the coronation of Joseph II as Holy Roman Emperor stimulated Goethe's interest in the present and his sense of the past. From the series of tutors engaged by his father he gained an unusual, if somewhat private education; in languages, at least, an excellent one. Insatiably curious, the boy gathered some inklings of the newer tendencies in literature, but Frankfurt was rather provincial, and his father's taste rigorously conservative. In *Poetry and Truth* is a delicious story of how Goethe and his sister, hidden behind a stove, declaimed some of Klopstock's more melodramatic hexameters in the room where their father was being shaved. Terrified, the poor barber spilled the shaving-dish over his client, and the literally dangerous book was formally forbidden.

At sixteen, Goethe left for the university at Leipzig, yielding to his father's insistence that he study law. With its famous university and well-established theater, Leipzig was less provincial than Frankfurt, and more of an intellectual center. There too, however, literary taste was rather conservative, the style of life was that of the old regime. Neither in his three years in Leipzig nor in the long stay at home following the breakdown which temporarily ended his studies did Goethe write anything of the first rank. His two brief dramas in Alexandrines contain clever turns of phrase and some sharp moral insights, but their main importance lay in their usefulness to the poet himself, as exercises in dramatic form. In the early lyrics—many of them, like the dramas, the product of his stay in Leipzig—there are to be sure a few lines which transcend the Rococo tradition, like

>Luna bricht die Nacht der Eichen
>Luna breaks the oak-trees' night

STORM AND STRESS

and others which show his unique sense of intimacy with nature, like the poem "Inconstancy," which parallels the flowing of a brook and the Heraclitan flux of human emotion; the smooth movement of the dactyls well symbolizes both:

> Im spielenden Bache da lieg ich, wie helle!
> Verbreite die Arme der kommenden Welle,
> Und buhlerisch drückt sie die sehnende Brust. . . .

> In the play of the brook there I'm lying—what glitter!
> I'm spreading my arms to the wave as it's coming,
> And wantonly pressing against my fond breast. . . .

Yet both these poems end, in true Rococo style, with epigrammatic, indeed frivolous, turns of phrase. While there are several places where the reader can discern the Goethean individuality, he would probably pay little attention to these verses unless he were aware of Goethe's later poetry.

In Strasbourg, in his twenty-first year, Goethe really became a great poet. (He had gone there to resume his interrupted law studies; as in Leipzig, he managed to keep the law from interfering with his genuine interests.) There is something very fitting in the fact that this took place in a region politically French, culturally largely German; it is consonant with Goethe's own role as a good European. To be sure, Goethe and his German friends at the university were cultural nationalists—he even thought that Gothic architecture was German—but their nationalism was free of any hatred and almost completely unpolitical. The name of Goethe's Alsatian love, Friederike

Brion, neatly symbolizes the dual, Franco-German character of the attractive provincial civilization which flourished between the Rhine and the Vosges. In this pleasant province the poet had time to admire the cathedral, read "Ossian" and Shakespeare, collect folk songs in the villages of the countryside, and pay court to the charming Friederike. Goethe, only recently escaped from the long convalescence at home which had followed his serious illness some two years before, was filled with a new sense of vigorous health. The experience of recovery after a crisis or defeat recurred frequently in his life. Often it appears in his works, most notably in the healing of Orestes in *Iphigenia in Tauris,* and in Faust's revival in the Alpine meadows. This motif of rebirth is closely linked with Goethe's belief—surely extrapolated from his own life—that men of genius often undergo repeated periods of puberty.

During his Alsatian days it was not the cathedral, the landscape, or even love which did the most to shape Goethe, but a "lived cultural experience" to borrow a term of Friedrich Gundolf's—his encounter with Johann Gottfried Herder. Herder was one of the most fertile and provocative thinkers of a rich century. Only five years older than Goethe, he was an omnivorous reader, vastly more informed than the younger man. More importantly, he was a full generation ahead of him intellectually, at the time of their first meeting. Goethe was still living, as it were, in the world of the Rococo and of eighteenth-century sentimentalism; Herder was already in the front rank of the *avant-garde*. His ideals were nature, original genius, the national spirit, folk poetry; his literary idols

STORM AND STRESS

were Shakespeare, Hebrew literature, "Ossian," Pindar, Homer, the Greek tragedians. In his *Fragments on German Literature* and *Critical Forests* he had proved himself to be a most stimulating, if not always truly critical, critic.

Herder was fortunate enough to find two great teachers in the remote Baltic provinces where he spent his youth: Kant and Johann Georg Hamann. The latter, perhaps the most difficult of German authors, was already famous as the "Magus of the North" for his Delphic utterances. One of the most violent opponents of the Enlightenment, he emphasized the non-rational forces in language, poetry, and life. Poetry, he believed, was "the original language of the human race." Simultaneously with Edward Young, he proclaimed in 1759 the dogma of original genius and subjected the neo-classic doctrine of imitation to bitter, if opaque scorn. Man can act authentically, Hamann maintained, only with the totality of his united energies. (He himself combined a powerful if erratic mind with religious awareness and a marked sensuality.) Man's nature is a whole, he held, and cannot be divided into the neat categories of "faculty psychology."

To return to Herder: when Goethe met him, he was undergoing a protracted and painful treatment following an eye operation; he was understandably irritable. Possibly he was envious of the charm and wealth of the younger man; perhaps also he sensed that Goethe would prove far more creative than he. At any rate, the poet did not let himself be put off by sarcasms; he realized how much Herder had to teach him. Inspired by Herder, he collected folk songs in the Alsatian villages, translated bits of "Ossian," wrote eloquent evocations of Gothic architecture and of Shakespeare, and soon produced the first version of a (more or less) Shakespearean drama, *Götz von Berlichingen*. Despite his resentments, Herder played the role of the John the Baptist of German letters.

The new spirit found expression in two of Goethe's early prose pieces which tell us a great deal about his frame of mind, his conception of genius, and the attitude of his generation. His speech "For Shakespeare's Day" (1771) was written for the first celebration of Shakespeare ever held in Germany; it took place in his parents' house in Frankfurt. Goethe declares himself eager to subordinate himself to the greater poet: he would be only too glad to play Pylades to Shakespeare's Orestes. More significant is his analysis of Shakespeare's plots:

> ... they are no plots at all, in the usual sense, but they all revolve around the secret point which no philosopher has yet seen or determined, in which the particularity of our ego, the freedom which our will claims, collides with the necessary course of the whole.

This sense of fate, soon to be strengthened by the study of Spinoza, was to play a great part in shaping Goethe's view of life, and his writings. Another quotation gives us an insight into the style of life of Goethe's generation:

> And I shout "Nature! nature!"
> Shakespeare's people have more of nature than anyone else.
> Then they all jump at my throat.
> Give me air, so that I can breathe!
> He competed with Prometheus, imitated his people stroke for stroke, but on a colossal scale—that is why we fail to recog-

nize our brothers; and then he gave life to them all by the breath of his spirit, he speaks through all of them, and one recognizes that all are interrelated.

The motif of Prometheus links Goethe's address on Shakespeare with his unfortunately entitled "On German Architecture" (1772). At the end of Goethe's vindication of the Gothic, he again invokes the demigod who links gods with men; the great architect has the same task. Goethe intended this rhapsodic tribute to the Strasbourg cathedral as a polemic against the neo-classic theories of a certain Laugier and an expression of spontaneous creativity. Characteristic expression, the poet maintained, is more important than abstract principles. In the circumstances, it is the more remarkable that Goethe discerned the classic virtues—simplicity, greatness, and unity—in the cathedral; he wrote as a crypto-classicist, *malgré-lui*. When he claimed that the style of the great church was German, his intention was not chauvinistic: it had been designed by Erwin von Steinbach, and the young enthusiast had never seen Chartres or Rheims.

It was in Alsace that Goethe really found himself as a lyric poet. The poems of those days show his gradual emergence from the Rococo tradition. Thus his "Awaken, Friederike" still speaks of the "night / Which one of your glances / Turns to day"; but conceits of this type are soon abandoned. The poems also show how he used the impulses of the folk song—he collected a dozen of them for Herder—and transformed them into his own lyric mode, managing to preserve the freshness and directness of the old songs while avoiding their sudden leaps in narration, undue repetitiousness, and occasional coarseness. His art here is one of concentration: he distilled the lyric "Wild Rose" out of a long, rather mediocre sixteenth-century folk song.

Most striking in these poems is their new dynamism of language. We can hardly share Goethe's personal, direct relationship to nature, still less accept his belief that "she" is loving and good; but the sheer force of his language—especially his verbs and his bold compounds—makes the change in our point of view toward nature almost irrelevant. One thinks of stanzas like two in his "May Song":

> Es dringen Blüten
> Aus jedem Zweig,
> Und tausend Stimmen
> Aus dem Gesträuch, . . .
>
> Du segnest herrlich
> Das frische Feld,
> Im Blütendampfe
> Die volle Welt.

Blossoms press forth / from every branch / and a thousand voices / from the undergrowth. . . . You bless with splendor / the new field, / in its aura of blossoms / the full world.

Perhaps the most powerful of these lyrics is "Welcome and Departure," with its amazing images:

> Mir schlug das Herz; geschwind zu Pferde,
> Und fort, wild, wie ein Held zur Schlacht!
> Der Abend wiegte schon die Erde,
> Und an den Bergen hieng die Nacht; .

STORM AND STRESS

> Schon stund im Nebelkleid die Eiche,
> Ein aufgethürmter Riese, da
> Wo Finsterniss aus dem Gesträuche
> Mit hundert schwarzen Augen sah.

> My heart beat high. At once, to horse! / And off, keen as a hero to battle. / Evening was already rocking earth to sleep / and night clung to the mountainsides. / Already the oak stood in its garment of clouds / a towering giant / where darkness from the undergrowth / gazed with its hundred dark eyes.

Hundreds of Goethe's lyrics—and many of his other works—were written to or about actual persons, as his famous statement that all his writings were "fragments of a great confession" clearly implies; and German scholars have been assiduous and successful in supplying us with an overwhelming mass of biographical facts. This puts the commentator in a real dilemma. If he explains the personal background in full, as has so often been done, he is likely to degrade the poetry to versified autobiography; yet completely to ignore it, in the instances when it sheds light on the work, would be willful obscurantism. There seems to be a sensible way out. When the poet mentions a "Friederike," a "Lili," a "Charlotte," why not satisfy the normal curiosity of the reader? Furthermore, some—though by no means all—of the many women Goethe loved were interesting and important people in their own right, like Charlotte von Stein and Marianne von Willemer, the latter a poet herself; they can hardly be passed over in complete silence.

When Goethe left Friederike Brion, to whom he seems to have been half-engaged, his sense of guilt was bitter and sharp. It is no accident that faithless lovers play a great part in his early works: in *Götz, Stella, Clavigo, Faust*. Actually, Goethe did only what millions of other young men, before and since, have done: he retreated from a promised, or half-promised, commitment when some interior voice told him that a permanent relationship was out of the question. (His fairy tale, "The New Melusina," casts light on this matter: it treats the passion of a grown man for a lovely and charming, but doll-sized, woman.) Goethe was no "great lover"[*] in the popular sense, still less a Casanova. Rather, he suffered from a strong, somewhat neurotic fear of marriage: he abandoned not only the simple Friederike but others who were more nearly his equals. One of them, Lili Schönemann, was apparently far more mature than he at the time of their engagement.

To return to literature: in the early 1770's Goethe was rapidly becoming an exemplar of what was soon to be called the Storm and Stress spirit. Generally, the young writers of this movement drew heavily on Hamann, Herder, and Rousseau. For Goethe, perhaps the central tenet of Storm and Stress was individualism: one was a free person oneself, despising rules and conventions, and one revered the great men, the geniuses, of history and legend. Thus Goethe turned increasingly to figures like Faust, Prometheus, Mohammed, and Caesar—and, on a lower plane, to the sixteenth-century knight Götz von Berlichingen, who was no superman but a sturdy, vigorous fellow, a *Kerl*. Similarly, the poet's imagination was

[*] See Theodor Reik's psychoanalytic study, *Fragment of a Great Confession* (New York, 1949).

STORM AND STRESS

drawn to "daemonic" superwomen, beyond good and evil. (He portrayed one in *Götz,* in the irresistible Adelheid, though he normally was more attracted by simple, unspoiled girls like Gretchen in *Faust.*) A polar type of hero was Werther, anything but a strong man but a sort of passive genius in his sensitivity and in the richness of his emotions.

The young Storm-and-Stress writers believed passionately that feeling and "the heart" were far superior to reason. "We wanted to live, not learn." Spontaneity was all. Often, Goethe would rise from bed in the middle of the night and dash down some inspiration in such haste that the lines slanted wildly across the page. Finding that the scratching of his pen distracted him, he substituted a pencil. In the early poetry, the warm inner glow (*Glut*) or fire of true creativity is a frequent motif. Everything must come from within:

> Ach, dass die innre Schöpfungskraft
> Durch meinen Sinn erschölle!
> Dass eine Bildung voller Saft
> Aus meinen Fingern quölle!

Ah, that the inner creative power / were ringing through my mind! / That a form instinct with life / were springing from my fingers!

The Storm and Stress spirit dominates Goethe's first major drama, *Götz von Berlichingen* (1773). Using the old knight's autobiography as his main source, the poet expressed in this colorful play the ideals he had just learned, his admiration for a German past characterized by loyalty and freedom, and his ambition to write an untrammeled play in Shakespeare's manner. Goethe's Götz—he called him "one of the noblest Germans"—is natural, honest, and very naive. One of the last of the free knights, Götz is fated to live in the age when the growing power of the princes, the adoption of Roman law, the whole regularization of society make his virtues increasingly untimely. (Following Herder and the eighteenth-century historian Justus Möser, Goethe regarded the period from which Götz sprang as a time of manly virtue, loyalty, and freedom, as peculiarly "German," in other words. While Goethe admired the Reformation, he depicted the spirit of the sixteenth century, against which Götz struggles in vain, as too rationalistic and unfeeling.) Götz battles against great odds, defying princes, bishops, treacherous nobles, and fat burghers. Placed in a tragic dilemma during the Peasants' War, he violates his oath by taking over the leadership of the rebels to prevent them from committing further atrocities. Broken by his ensuing sense of guilt, by betrayals, the death of friends, and above all by his sense that an evil time has come over the world, he dies with the word "freedom" on his lips. His weak friend Weislingen, torn between his fiancée and the daemonic superwoman Adelheid, affords a contrast to Götz's sturdy virtue. In depicting Weislingen and many another character, Goethe wrote to purge himself of a sense of malaise or guilt—felt, in this instance, for his chameleon-like inconstancy toward the girl he loved and yet was impelled finally to forsake.

Its action extending over seven years, *Götz von Berlichingen* becomes dangerously epic toward the end. In fact, we see Götz's gradual loss of self-confidence develop almost as in a novel. Generally, one cannot depart from the dramatic unities without paying a price for it. Goethe let the action roam freely over the countryside—there were fifty-seven scenes in the first version*—and did not manage to keep his hero always in the focus of attention. What unity the play has lies in its tone and in Götz's character.

Upon reading the first draft, Herder wrote to Goethe, with characteristic severity: "Shakespeare has ruined you completely." Coming from the champion of Shakespeare, the comment seems paradoxical as well as harsh; but when one recalls that Goethe at this time regarded Shakespeare's work as a peep show or kaleidoscope, one can see what Herder meant. Fascinated by the breadth, variety, and color of Shakespeare's world, Goethe failed to emulate the dramatic thrust and power of his work; but he shows an affinity to his model in his sense of fate and his avoidance of pat "poetic justice," his introduction of the stock character of the witty court fool, his use of quibbles and songs. Goethe reveals a further debt: the racy, drastic language owes as much to Luther's Bible as to the Elizabethan.

Götz first made Goethe famous in Germany; in fact it brought forth a swarm of imitations, the "knight-and-robber dramas" and popular novels of the same type, which the poet heartily disliked. While it is scarcely one of his great achievements, it first demonstrated how richly he was endowed—in characterization, mastery of color

* It was written in 1771 but not published until 1832.

and rhythm in dialogue, ability to evoke landscape and atmosphere. Possibly the most memorable of the many scenes are the uncanny ones: Götz's encounter with the gypsies, when he is wandering in defeat, rather like Lear on the blasted heath; and the frightening session of the secret court or *Femgericht,* at which the judges take the law into their own hands and condemn the daemonic Adelheid to death for her sins. (Ironically, this scene, through its imitation by Walter Scott, seems to have provided the Ku-Klux Klan with a model for its sinister councils.)

More strongly and explicitly than in *Götz,* the spirit of the literary revolution is expressed in a succession of free-verse hymns, mainly set in short, dynamic lines, written in the early 1770's. They center on the figure of the genius—as demigod, creator, or religious hero—and the closely linked theme of poetic creativity. "Wanderer's Storm Song," which Goethe later too harshly characterized as "half-nonsense," is a monologue dramatizing the struggle to find inspiration; it ends in exhausted defeat.

In contrast, Goethe's triumphant "Mohammed's Song" shows the religious genius in the image of a stream, born in the mountains, joined by lesser brooks (his "brethren"), which forces its way through the desert, brings abundance and splendor to all, and meets its father, the "eternal ocean." The final lines show the power and the beneficence of the great river, whose waters are literally those of life, just as the "father" is clearly God:

> Unaufhaltsam rauscht er weiter,
> Lässt der Türme Flammengipfel,

STORM AND STRESS

> Marmorhäuser, eine Schöpfung
> Seiner Fülle, hinter sich.
>
> Zedernhäuser trägt der Atlas
> Auf den Riesenschultern; sausend
> Wehen über seinem Haupte
> Tausend Flaggen durch die Lüfte,
> Zeugen seiner Herrlichkeit.
>
> Und so trägt er seine Brüder,
> Seine Schätze, seine Kinder,
> Dem erwartenden Erzeuger
> Freudebrausend an das Herz.

Unresisted he flows further / leaves the towers' flaming peaks, / marble houses, a creation / of his plenty, at his back. / An Atlas, he carries cedar houses / on his giant shoulders; rustling / fly above his head / a thousand banners through the breezes / witnesses of his splendor. / And he carries so his brothers, his possessions, his children / joy-resounding, into the arms / of his awaiting father.

It is significant that the religious founder displays none of the self-absorption of the superman—a word Goethe used only ironically. The relation between river and ocean is reciprocal: each longs for the other. (Similarly, in the somewhat later hymn "Ganymede," an amazing expression of man's sense of unity with God and nature, the youth feels himself embracing and embraced by the "all-loving Father.") Most striking of all is the bold use, in "Mohammed's Song," of magnificent compounds: "brother-fountains," "snake-like-winding" (to represent the river's course), "silver-splendid," "joy-resounding."

Possibly even more powerful is the most famous of these hymns, "Prometheus," which Georg Brandes called the greatest revolutionary poem in world literature. That it may well be, but the revolution intended here is not political, but artistic, ethical, and religious; it stands also for the eternal revolt of sons against fathers. The defiant Prometheus who appears here is primarily the artist, who forms men in his own image, men who will suffer and rejoice, experiencing like Faust the whole of existence, ignoring the arrogant and indifferent Olympians. A strongly humanistic note prevails: embittered, disillusioned with the gods, Prometheus will keep his gaze fixed on this world, trusting his own creative powers. After all, there are forces mightier than Zeus:

> Hat nicht mich zum Manne geschmiedet
> Die allmächtige Zeit
> Und das ewige Schicksal,
> Meine Herrn und deine?

<small>Was I not forged into a man by / almighty time / and eternal fate, / my lords and yours?</small>

Fascinated as he was by the myth of Prometheus, Goethe also devoted a fragmentary drama to the demigod (1773). Again Prometheus is the creator in revolt; with the help of Minerva, he has given his statues self-reliant life, and the fragment depicts the founding of a new civilization. One striking passage anticipates the whole *Liebestod* tradition from Novalis to Mann. Prometheus is instructing his daughter Pandora: "When from the depths of your inmost being / You feel, utterly shaken, every-

STORM AND STRESS

thing / That you have ever experienced, in joy or sorrow ... And you seem to lose all sense of your own being / And sink down, and all around you / Sinks into night, and you in your own inner feeling / Embrace a world / Then man dies." Naturally enough, the innocent Pandora wishes to die at once. In the drama, Jupiter is no tyrant but a far-seeing, tolerant ruler, and there is a hint of an eventual peace to be made between Prometheus and the gods. In a later fragment, "Pandora's Return," (see below pp. 106–108) all hostility has vanished. Goethe's statement, "I'm not born to be a tragic poet, since my nature is conciliatory" contains an important element of the truth though by no means all of it.

"Eagle and Dove," an ironic fable in free verse, is anything but conciliatory. A young eagle, crippled by an arrow, can no longer soar; bound to earth, he is eating out his heart. His would-be comforter, a dove, points out to him the safety and convenience of the humble life: be content and you'll be happy. But the wounded genius has only scorn for the bourgeois common sense of the "sensible" dove.

One measure of Goethe's extraordinary vitality and basic psychological health is that he was able to stand back from himself, view his works and his contemporaries objectively, and make lighthearted fun, when the mood took him, of his most cherished beliefs. Even in the most critical times, when he often felt like one pursued by the Furies, as his letters show us, he had this ability for what might be called comic catharsis. A series of skits, verses, and farces shows this side of him; the most remarkable is the brief verse play *Satyros* (1773). This brilliant little drama is both a satire and a satyr play: it represents Goethe's reckoning with the Storm and Stress, with Herder, Hamann, Rousseau—and himself. The satyr expounds the cult of nature and love with demagogic power: he brainwashes the simple folk so effectively that they join in his ecstatic vegetarian chant: "Raw chestnuts / Marvelous grub!" Before long, the satyr is caught attempting rape and has to leave town, but the gentle maiden Psyche will follow him; the soul cannot resist the appeal of the body. Yet if the time's belief in "nature" is mocked, it is also glorified; the satyr's dithyrambic lines have real poetic power. A certain *healthy* ambivalence pervades the play.

Satyros is at the farthest possible extreme from Goethe's *The Sorrows of Young Werther* (1774). Largely composed of Werther's letters, it follows the tradition of Richardson's novels and Rousseau's *La nouvelle Héloïse;* but it is brief and concentrated where they are wordy, focused on the letters of a single correspondent where the earlier epistolary novels include those of several writers. In the relatively happy first part of *Werther*, the tone owes much to Goldsmith's idylls; the second half is imbued with the darkness of English poets of the "graveyard school" and the melancholy of "Ossian."

There is little to say about the external action of the novel. Young Werther—sensitive, attractive, very much the man of feeling—has left his family and home to avoid an embarrassing situation: a girl has fallen in love with him, and he feels partly to blame. In his retreat, a town surrounded by a paradisiacal countryside, he soon meets and falls in love with Lotte, who is already betrothed to

STORM AND STRESS

the worthy Albert. (It is indicated, and made quite clear in Goethe's later revision of the novel, that Werther was "difficult" and labile *before* he met her.) After a spring and summer of "Platonic" bliss with Lotte, mingled with increasing envy of Albert, Werther tears himself away. In the second part Werther, attempting a practical career at court, is severely snubbed (because of his middle-class origin) and resigns. In the fall of the following year, he returns—against his better judgment—to the town where Lotte and Albert live; they have now married. He becomes increasingly envious and miserable, believes that Lotte would have been happier had she married him, and learns belatedly (from a dream) that his passion for her is now unmistakably a sexual one. Albert becomes increasingly jealous; Lotte, upset; Werther's depression is further darkened by a series of incidents involving minor personages. At a last scene with Lotte, in Albert's absence, he embraces her; she is stirred but remains virtuously firm. Having borrowed Albert's pistols from her on the ambiguous pretext that he needs them for a "journey," he commits suicide shortly before Christmas, during the longest night of the year. Simple workmen carry his body to be buried. "No clergyman accompanied him."

In the year after *Werther* was published, Goethe stated that he had represented in his novel "a young man, gifted with deep, unspoiled sensitivity and penetrating insight, who loses himself in visionary dreams, undermines himself by empty speculations until finally, deranged by unhappy passions he experiences, especially an unending love, he puts a bullet in his head." One notes that while love is an important factor, it is not the first or basic cause. Much later, Goethe maintained that *Werther* had no didactic purpose. In a sense, this is undoubtedly true; but to portray a suicide with such empathy and power, to contrast the delicate, charismatic young man to the unfeeling worlds of bourgeois respectability and aristocratic pride, was a defiant challenge to the age.

There is a deep ambivalence in the presentation of Werther. To be sure, he is certainly a "weak hero," one of the tribe of Rousseau's St. Preux. Goethe himself underlined his failings, his emotional self-indulgence: "I cherish my heart like a sick child," Werther says. It is easy for a post-Freudian generation to spot him as a neurotic, though one must beware of anachronistic judgments. But on balance, Werther is certainly intended as an appealing, basically admirable character—though not a model. His very name implies that he is more valued and valuable (*werter*) than the common run of men. He has the Storm-and-Stress scorn of rules in literature and of etiquette in life. His pantheistic feeling for nature, his intuitive insight into poetry, are both close to Goethe's own. He is drawn to children and simple people, though it is doubtful how much he really has in common with the humble folk he praises. When he decides to commit suicide, he is partly altruistic—he wants to further Lotte's happiness on earth; partly selfish—he persuades himself that he will be united with her in the life to come. To some extent, he is associated with Christ, particularly when he calls for bread and wine before his death. In his strength and his weakness, he represents that German inwardness which flourished in the Pietist movement and was secularized by eighteenth-century sentimentalism. "I turn back into myself and find a world," is his most revealing statement. From a sociological point of view, the middle-class German intellectual almost had to turn back within himself; unlike his French and British contemporaries, he had hardly any other place to go.

Lotte, young, pretty, motherly, and sensitive enough to understand Werther, has an irresistible appeal for him. Whether she is cutting bread for her younger brothers and sisters or demonstrating her rapport with Werther by sharing his reminiscences of a famous poem of Klopstock's, she fulfills his ideal. Like so many of Goethe's characters, she is both guiltless and guilty. Doubtless Werther would have perished even without her, but she does, however unconsciously, encourage his passion; that it is she who hands him the pistols is symbolically right.

Of course, Goethe drew heavily on his own experiences —he did not even change the first name of the historical Lotte—as well as those of an acquaintance who committed suicide. The line between Werther and Goethe is very thin, as has been pointed out. But Werther is only one side of Goethe: the poet himself, at this time, was writing robust, vigorous poems like "The Wandering Jew" and a series of earthy farces. Basically, Goethe had a Spinozan sense of self-preservation—*conatus sese preservandi*—which saw him through the many Wertherean moods that assailed him in the course of his life.

I have already referred to the symmetry of *Werther*. His passion rises during the spring and summer; he moves toward death in the autumn and winter. When happy he reads Homer; in his distraction he revels in "Ossian." Motifs of hope in the first part become symbols of despair in the second. Skillful use is made of anticipation, as in Werther's debate with Albert about suicide, and of parallelism: two other characters are driven to despair by unrequited love. Werther's own hyperemotional approach to life is implicitly contrasted to the attitude of the recipient of his letters and of the editor who reports the last day of his life. Amazing richness and variety have been compressed into a novel of not much more than 100 pages.

Above all, it is the expressivity and range of Goethe's language when transmuted into art material which in itself might seem sentimental, morbid, or merely trivial. When Werther helps a young peasant girl at the well, the style is appropriately simple and patriarchal; it can soar in a rush of pantheistic feeling, and express the depths of dejection when the illusion of oneness with nature has passed. Early in the book his experience of "God-in-nature" recalls Ganymede's:

> When mist is rising in my dear valley around me, and the sun at its height does not shine into my wood's impenetrable darkness, and only single rays steal into the holy place within, and I lie in the tall grass by the falling brook and observe a thousand varied leaves of grass closer to the earth; when I feel closer to my heart the teeming of the little world between the stalks, . . . and feel the presence of the Almighty who created us in His own image, the breath of the All-loving One, who bears and preserves us, soaring in eternal bliss; my friend! when my eyes then grow dim and the world around me and the sky are all at rest in my soul, like the figure of a loved one —then I often think, yearningly: "Oh, if you could express that, if you could express on paper what lives so abundantly, so warmly in you, so that it would be the mirror of your soul as your soul is the mirror of the infinite God!"

STORM AND STRESS

How typical of Werther to pour out his feelings about nature and God, and his unfocused ambition to write, in one breathless sentence!

Yet at the end, the language is as curt as Hemingway's:

> At twelve noon he died. The presence of the bailiff and his arrangements prevented a crowd. At about eleven at night he had him buried at the place which he had chosen; the old man followed the body, as did his sons. Albert was not able to. People feared for Lotte's life. Workmen carried him. No clergyman accompanied him.

The tremendous success of *Werther* overwhelmed and rather appalled Goethe. The book was banned in some parts of Germany, parodied, and defended; there was talk of "Werther fever" and "Werther illness"; young men dressed *à la* Werther; suicides were attributed to the impact of the book. The poet felt impelled to end a brief poem about his novel with the line "Be a man and do not follow me." In the revision published in 1787 he took pains to make Werther more conscious of his drift toward death, thus increasing his responsibility and diminishing Lotte's. Among the many novels which later imitated *Werther* in some degree are Ugo Foscolo's *The Last Letters of Jacopo Ortis*, Chateaubriand's *René*; Senancour's *Obermann*, and Constant's *Adolphe*. While the contemporary German imitations are not impressive, a long line of sensitive heroes is in his debt, from Hölderlin's Hyperion to Mann's Tonio Kröger and even, in a sense, Kafka's unhappy bug, Gregor Samsa. Tactfully presented, *Werther*, which has become almost a symbol of sentimentality, can interest and often touch even tough-minded readers of our own time.

3. RESOLUTION AND FIRST MATURITY

IN HIS EARLY AND MIDDLE TWENTIES, GOETHE WAS STILL A young man of marked instability. To his friends he was known as "the wanderer"; he did move about the countryside a great deal, but the real force of this epithet is symbolic. Often he compared himself to a chameleon. He had little interest in his profession and seems to have practiced law very casually. Public opinion classed him with the wild young men, the *Genies*. To a dangerous extent, he was the prey of shifting moods: now that of Werther, now of Faust. There were happier hours, of course, when he could identify himself with Prometheus or Mohammed. Although *Werther* proved a tremendous success, Goethe was by no means sure that he was intended to be only, or primarily, a writer. His relations with women showed an especially mercurial side: he was highly inflammable but had a real dread of marriage; the sense of "guiltless guilt" was very real—and was a strong incentive to poetry, not only lyrical. "If I didn't write dramas, I would perish,"

RESOLUTION AND FIRST MATURITY

he exclaimed. The road to any sort of peace, to inner balance, was a painful one.

During the year after Goethe had made Lotte famous by publishing *Werther*, the name of another girl, Lili, figured in his lyrics. Without going into biographical detail, one can say that attraction and repulsion, the need for freedom and the necessity of love, dominate these poems; they are filled with images of bondage and of escape. "Lili's Park" is strikingly ambivalent; for all the humor of these verses, they are marked by real bitterness. Lili appears as a Circe; her admirers make up a menagerie; the poet himself is the bear, "unlicked, untrained," bound to the enchantress by a magic silk thread. Lili's world is that of Rococo etiquette, nicely symbolized by "porcelain Oreads" and her teasing use of French phrases; the bear is a rebellious outsider. At the end he vows to escape: "I feel, I swear, I've still the power." More courteous in attitude, the poem "To Belinda" omits invective but still contrasts the artificial world of society, with its glittering chandeliers and the "unendurable faces" of its aristocratic gamblers, to the natural sphere in which the poet had previously lived. A later poem, beginning "Souvenir of vanished joy," treats the relationship to Lili as ended but returns to the image of the magic bond or thread; the poet will never be really free again: he still drags a bit of the thread around with him, like a bird which has escaped but will never forget its captivity.

The prose drama *Stella* (1776) is thematically related to these poems: it too deals with the struggle between love and the male's half-guilty attempts to preserve his freedom. In this rather minor work the protagonist Fernando is torn between an older and a younger woman. Both of them he has deserted, but both still love him; at the end, he is rewarded with—both. For the older Goethe, this was too much: in his revision of 1805, Fernando and the soulful young Stella both die; but applying severe moral standards to *Stella* is breaking a butterfly upon the wheel. As a period piece, full of graceful apostrophes to feeling and "the heart," the play has a certain charm.

Far more important was the change which was taking place in Goethe's lyrics. Gradually, in a few poems, he was moving from the subjective "heart-outpourings" of the Storm and Stress toward a more objective mode of expression. It is a shift rather like that which Rilke made in the school of Rodin, from subjectivity to his *Dinggedichte* ("thing-poems"). "On the Lake" moves through three distinct moods in its twenty lines, and yet preserves, as Staiger has noted, an essential unity. The first stanza expresses the literally biological sense of union with nature which Goethe had in his youth: as the skiff moves across the lake, surrounded by mountains, the lyrical "I" of the poem draws "nourishment from the world through his umbilical cord." A second very brief "movement"—its shift to trochaics indicating unrest— introduces memories of the past which might distract him; they are curtly dismissed. In the final section the focus changes from the poet to the objective world:

> Morgenwind umflügelt
> Die beschattete Bucht,
> Und im See bespiegelt
> Sich die reifende Frucht.

RESOLUTION AND FIRST MATURITY

> Morning wind spreads its wings about / the shadowed bay, / and the ripening fruit / is mirrored in the lake.

The closing anticipates Stefan George's famous onomatopoetic line: "Und reife Früchte auf den Boden klopfen —And ripe fruits fall pounding on the ground." The final image of ripening fruit symbolizes the process that the poem, like the poet, has gone through; the "mirroring" of the lake reflects the function of poetry, which is now to mirror, not merely to express. Similarly, while the poem "Autumnal Feeling" ends on the subjective note implied in the title, it starts with a protracted, concrete image of the maturing vine, beginning:

> Fetter grüne, du Laub
> Am Rebengeländer
> Hier mein Fenster herauf . . .
>
> Green more richly, you leaves,
> On the vine-covered trellis
> By my windowpanes here!

Another unrhymed poem of the period, "Voyage," evokes the excitement of departure, the fears of friends, and the dangers of the journey. Yet the traveler stands at the helm like a man; wind and waves play with the ship, not with his heart. Whether he is to be shipwrecked or make harbor, he maintains his trust in his gods. The stoic resolution expressed here tells a great deal about Goethe's mood around the time of his departure for Weimar.

The drama *Egmont*, presumably begun about this time, is perhaps most interesting as an expression of Goethe's gradually emergent view of life: how is a man to live in a way which will enable him to defy care and anxiety, to acknowledge the power of fate without trembling before it? At its inception, it is generally believed, *Egmont* was very close to *Götz von Berlichingen* in intention: a quasi-historical drama concerned with questions of freedom, with an admirable hero who tends to be too trustful in his relations with other men. But it took Goethe a long while to finish *Egmont*—the play was finally published in 1788—and in the completed work, the inner action becomes more important than the outer, as is so often the case in Goethe's dramas. While there are colorful mass scenes and several conflicts between sharply defined characters, Egmont's inner struggle and his personality as such are of paramount interest.

Perhaps the central theme of *Egmont* is the Spinozan "Remember to live!" In this sense the young Count Egmont is more deeply concerned with warding off fear and worry than with the mere preservation of his life or even with the defense of his Dutch countrymen against Spanish tyranny. Not that he is indifferent to the common cause, but political freedom is of secondary value—a very German attitude. Like his great antagonist, Alba, he has a keen awareness of the power of destiny; but his fatalism, unlike the Spaniard's, is neither harsh nor gloomy:

> . . . I have not yet reached the pinnacle of my growth, and if some day I stand upon it, I will stand firmly, not anxiously. If I am destined to fall, then let a thunderbolt, a stormy wind, yes, a mistaken step of my own dash me downwards into the abyss—there I'll lie among many thousands. I have never disdained, even for a small prize, to cast the bloody die of war

with my good comrades; and should I show myself a miser when it's a matter of the whole free worth of life?

Egmont's faithful secretary feels that such words reveal *hubris,* and perhaps they do, but this resolute carefreeness accounts for much of his attractiveness. In his monumental *Goethe,* Gundolf links Egmont's attitude with the poet's own sense, at the time, that nothing really evil could happen to him. This is persuasive, but one must not forget that he was subject in these years to a very different mood as well: that of Orestes. Egmont is genuinely charismatic, adored by the people and his soldiers, admired by the other nobles. Only Alba, his one equal in the play, can resist him; and even here, Egmont wins a symbolic victory by charming his opponent's son. Yet he must pay the price of political futility for the privilege of remaining always sanguine and buoyant. Not Egmont but the "contrast-figure'" William of Orange, who studies politics like a chess game, is the savior of his people, though Goethe's ending rather smudges this point.

The political burden of the play is carried mainly by the great discussion between Egmont and Alba in the fourth act. In its confrontation of humane liberal and dedicated fanatic, this scene anticipates two other famous conflicts in German literature: the clash in Büchner's *Danton's Death* between the hero and Robespierre, and the debates between Settembrini and Naphta in Mann's *The Magic Mountain.* (That the liberal is practically defeated though morally victorious in two cases out of three—the outcome is less clear-cut in *The Magic Mountain*—reflects light on the course of German history.)

Egmont is anything but a radical: he is a liberal conservative or conservative liberal, who defends the ordered freedom of self-respecting burghers. (One should note that while Goethe abhorred the French Revolution, he admired the American, which was taking place at about the time when he was writing *Egmont*.) As in *Julius Caesar*, the populace as such is anything but impressive. Above all, Egmont believes that the individuality, the peculiar political and religious traditions of a nation, must be respected; the people should be led, not driven. The contrast between protagonist and antagonist is reinforced by that between easygoing Netherlanders and rigidly disciplined Spaniards: Alba's troops are like "machines in which a devil is sitting."

Egmont's mistress Clara is a simple, unspoiled girl—a Gretchen type so to speak: she seems to embody "nature" in his eyes. In their relation one encounters a new attitude toward sexual matters: it is "free love" without a bad conscience; indeed, Clara glories in it. (When Goethe later wrote that he had freed his countrymen from the "nets of the Philistines," he had moral liberation in mind.)

At one point, Egmont appears to Clara in full court dress, with all his regalia, like Zeus to Semele. She requested this to be sure, but a certain Narcissism in him becomes evident. Egmont has taken Clara away, with no difficulty, from the miserable Brackenburg, a lower-middle-class Werther who fills pages with his *Weltschmerz*. Shortly before his execution, Egmont entrusts his beloved to a younger friend—"You won't scorn her because she was mine"—but Clara has already killed herself.

RESOLUTION AND FIRST MATURITY

With its mass scenes and broad scope, *Egmont* recalls a panoramic historical painting, but often the focus narrows down to two persons: Egmont with his secretary, with Clara, with Orange, with Alba. Like *Götz*, the drama takes its time, but some scenes, like the one showing Alba luring the hero into his trap, are full of action and tension. In the fourth and fifth acts, the rhythmical prose of the dialogue often approaches, and occasionally reaches, blank verse.

Appropriately enough, the most incisive critic of *Egmont* was Schiller, the master of historical tragedy in German. His review of the drama rightly emphasized that its unity lies solely in Egmont's character, which is not that of a great man: he is a "benevolent, cheerful, openhearted person. . . ." An Egmont who deliberately forgets his patriotic responsibility in a visit to Clara is not really heroic. Finally, Schiller maintained, the last scene of the drama—a tableau displaying Egmont's last dream, with Clara in the role of the goddess of freedom inspiring the Dutch to heroic deeds—is a *"salto mortale* into the world of the opera."

Schiller's remarks have been found too stringent, and his own revision of *Egmont* was certainly no improvement on the original. Basically, however, he was in the right: one can accept Egmont as a hero perhaps, but not as a *political* hero; the ending is forced and unconvincing. Egmont's concept of freedom refers to his private world, not to that of history.

In the autumn of 1775 Goethe resolved to accept the invitation of the young Duke Karl August of Weimar to join his court. It was his first mature venture, the beginning of his career in the practical world. The decision was not entirely easy: there had been an irritating, though accidental delay in confirming the arrangement, and the poet's father warned him insistently against the dangers of aristocratic society. Writing a generation later, in *Poetry and Truth,* Goethe stressed the "daemonic" character of this event: his sense that it was determined by a higher power. Possibly he stylized his retrospective account, but it was indeed a fateful step. His whole way of living was radically changed; aside from his journeys, Weimar was his home for the rest of his life and the Duke his close friend, until the ruler's death, over fifty years later. Like Wilhelm Meister, he abandoned both the bourgeois and the Bohemian spheres to live in an aristocratic milieu. Inevitably this had its effect, though Weimar society was extraordinarily liberal for the time, and the Duke himself, in the first years, lived in an exuberant, unfettered way. Goethe never turned into a snob; while he came to respect convention, he never let it stand in the way of something he really wanted. But inevitably his elevation imparted a certain coolness to his manner, while giving him a broader range of vision. Schiller's lines about the poet who lives, like the king, "on the pinnacles of humanity" apply here. But the "Olympian" aspect of Goethe developed very gradually; for the time being he remained the irresistibly attractive, impulsive young genius who had charmed the Duke.

When Goethe arrived in Weimar, late in 1775, he found a small, rather unsightly, shabby town. For that matter, the whole Duchy was poverty-stricken. The town's population, throughout the century, remained stable at about

RESOLUTION AND FIRST MATURITY

6,000. While there were some pleasant gardens and parks and a busy market place, it was extremely unimpressive on the whole; Herder called it a "wretched cross between a capital city and a village." Until a new palace was dedicated in 1803, the ducal residences were very modest. Although Karl August's rule showed "patriarchal government at its best," it had its weaknesses; and there was no thought of granting democratic rights to the peasants and burghers. Gradually, however, the cultural renascence of the town began to change its appearance: a theater was built in 1780 and replaced by a larger one forty-five years later. More sanguine than Herder, Goethe could write that the little capital had "a special fate: like Bethlehem in Judea, small and great."

Modest though it was, Weimar could already boast one major literary figure when Goethe arrived—Wieland. He had recently been the target of one of Goethe's satiric farces, which reproached him for failure to understand either the Greeks or Shakespeare, for general superficiality and insincerity; but Wieland's mature tolerance and Goethe's charm obviated any ill-feeling. Herder arrived the following year and was made court preacher on Goethe's recommendation; Schiller came much later, around the turn of the century. An increasing number of lesser lights joined the constellation. By 1800, there was perhaps the greatest concentration of genius in Weimar that had existed in one place since Elizabethan London. On the other hand, local society tended to be stuffy; the theater was at first small and amateurish; while there was genuine enthusiasm for literature and the arts, the tone was largely set by women. Some of them were genuinely bright; others seem to have been blue-stockings, in the worst sense of the word. One of the most remarkable of these ladies, Charlotte von Stein, was to dominate Goethe's life for over a decade.

Thomas Mann well compared Goethe's rise to eminence and power to the success of young Joseph at Pharaoh's court. With meteoric speed he became Privy Legation Counselor with the right to vote in the cabinet and, a few years later, Minister; Karl August paid him an excellent salary and procured him a patent of hereditary nobility. Not everyone accepted him with Wieland's magnanimity. It was not merely a matter of envy; experienced officials could well be concerned when this wild young "original genius" was made one of the most powerful men of the state. They need not have worried: Goethe revealed an unsuspected conscientiousness, even in matters of detail. While he joined at first in the revels of the young Duke—which seem to have been untrammeled but in no sense vicious—he acted from motives of friendship and pedagogic tact: only through close association could he help to guide his ruler. The theme of *Bildung*, of education in and through life, became central to Goethe.

Bildung plays a great part in a novel Goethe worked on, and never finished, during his first decade at Weimar: *Wilhelm Meister's Theatrical Mission*. When Goethe wrote *Meister's Apprenticeship* (see pages 84–91) he revised the fragment drastically, using it as the basis for roughly the first half of his famous novel. But the *Theatrical Mission* is lively and interesting in its own right. The account of young Wilhelm's journeys is set in a picaresque tone which is gayer and more realistic than that of

RESOLUTION AND FIRST MATURITY

the completed novel. At the same time, the book is a microcosm of the development of the eighteenth-century German theater, from Wilhelm's boyish interest in puppet plays—an autobiographical touch—through the productions of amateur stages and a wandering troupe of actors, through Racine to Shakespeare, whose *Hamlet* is the symbol of the highest dramatic ideal. The novel is as much interested in the metamorphoses of the theater as in Wilhelm's. About its presumable intended ending, one can only guess: possibly Wilhelm was to learn, as he did in *Meister's Apprenticeship*, that he was a mere dilettante as an actor, but was to "find himself" as a dramatic poet, the German Shakespeare.

Meister's Theatrical Mission is close to Fielding in its style and view of life. In sharp contrast to *Werther*, the external world appears as very real; this is no expression of subjective feeling, but a picture of the world. Though the book is full of ironies, its title was surely meant seriously by Goethe—at least at its inception. Despite a certain roughness—sudden leaps in the narration, occasional use of dialect, etc.—the book is more nearly unified than *Meister's Apprenticeship*, more vigorous, less didactic. One regrets that the original version had no influence on the development of the novel; the manuscript disappeared, and the copy which was finally found (in Switzerland) did not turn up until 1910.

In its hearty robustness, *Meister's Theatrical Mission* is an exception to the general trend of Goethe's works of his early Weimar years. Most of them show the impact of Charlotte von Stein's personality and view of life. It is hard to discover what Frau von Stein was really like, especially since she destroyed her letters to Goethe after her break with him. To some extent, no doubt, he projected onto her qualities of which he felt the need. We do have certain facts: she was considerably older than Goethe, unbeautiful, unhappily married; with a tendency to introspection and melancholy. She was intelligent though not brilliant. Old-fashioned in her literary taste, she seems to have been rather a prude: she disapproved of Egmont's little Clara. But though the "real" Charlotte may have been less than entrancing, it is the poet's image of her that matters. She inspired many of his most famous lyrics; her healing power is symbolized in *Iphigenia,* her insistence on decorum in the character of the Princess in *Tasso;* she was the recipient of about fifteen hundred of his letters, some of which have the intrinsic value of poetry. He referred to her in his diaries as the sun, as gold; he associated her with the moon in his lyrics. After knowing Charlotte only a few months, he expressed in eloquent poetry his belief that she must have been his sister or his wife in a previous existence. It is not too much to say that she revolutionized his poetry and his *Weltanschauung,* though the regime she imposed was too ascetic to last indefinitely. At any rate, Goethe was fervently in love with her for years; she was his goddess, his muse.

On one plane, *Iphigenia in Tauris* (final version, 1787) is the concretion of two of Goethe's experiences: the sense of being guilt-laden, pursued by the Furies; and the almost miraculous feeling of recovered health after that obsessive dread has vanished. In a famous lyric, Goethe thanked Charlotte directly for having calmed and re-

RESOLUTION AND FIRST MATURITY

stored him; in the drama, Iphigenia is the savior of her brother Orestes. As in Euripides, Iphigenia (who had been miraculously preserved from death by Diana) is a priestess in remote Tauris; Goethe also has his Orestes come there with Pylades, to purge himself of guilt by stealing the statue of the goddess; he too has a moving recognition scene. Yet Goethe reshaped Euripides' plot very freely; where the Greek characters used trickery to gull the barbarians, he endowed his Orestes and Iphigenia with modern sensibility and Christian consciences. The objection that Goethe's personages are noble anachronisms, more German than Greek, is correct but largely irrelevant. From Vergil to Gide, writers have retold Greek myths from the point of view of their own times and nationalities. Thus Goethe's characters think in the cosmopolitan terms of the eighteenth century; his Iphigenia, "seeking the land of Hellas with her soul," expresses both his longing for the South and the spiritual inwardness of the Pietist tradition.

Written "against the theater," as Goethe later put it, the play has two decisive actions, both of which are ethical and psychological, not external. The poet called the healing of the matricide Orestes the "axis of the piece." On first appearance, he has reached a point beyond desperation; were it not for his friend Pylades, he would gladly be slain:

> It is the path of death that now we tread:
> At every step my soul grows more serene.

Encountering Iphigenia, whom he does not at first recognize, he finds himself unable to conceal his identity by lying—"Between us let there be truth!"—and he confesses his guilty past. (The motif of wagering one's whole existence on the truth will be repeated; it is paralleled by a famous line in Mozart's *The Magic Flute*). Orestes' healing has begun, but when his sister reveals *her* identity, he is still too confused and "sick" to believe her immediately. After swooning in exhaustion, he has a vision of entering Hades: he sees his murdered father and mother and the whole accursed family of Tantalus. They have forgiven each other; he can at last forgive himself. (The impact of Iphigenia's personality has led him to view their whole past differently: *interpretatio Christiana,* as is were. One should not understand the "cure" in purely Christian or in psychoanalytical terms, though it has analogies to both.) After Iphigenia's appeal to Apollo and Diana, Orestes' recovery is complete: he expresses an almost Faustian resolve to pursue "the joy of life and noble deeds."

Up to this point, Iphigenia has seemed almost superhumanly noble and virtuous. But she is not perfect; as Heinz Politzer has brilliantly shown, she has lived a withdrawn, isolated existence, "on an inner island surrounded by the outer island of Tauris." To save the lives of Orestes, Pylades, and herself, and to enable her brother to make off with the statue of Diana, she consents to tell a lie. This involves deceiving her benefactor, the well-meaning king of Tauris, and plunges her into a moral crisis of her own. For the moment, she reverts to the old belief in cruel, jealous gods and implacable fate; her song: "Oh, fear the immortals, You children of men!" strikes the most authentically "Greek" note of the play.

RESOLUTION AND FIRST MATURITY

Yet it is impossible for her to live by lying: she challenges the gods to prove that their true nature is beneficent, just as she has earlier cried in desperation: "Save me, and save your image in my soul!" These are heroic words, if full of unconscious arrogance from an orthodox point of view. Like Orestes, she gambles on complete truthfulness —and wins. The last difficulty is resolved when we learn that Apollo's words "Bring back the sister" were ambiguous, as Delphic utterances normally are: the god had Orestes' sister in mind, not the cultic statue of his own.

In form, structure, and language, *Iphigenia* shows a triple heritage. As noted, it is indebted to Racine in its stress on inner action, its symmetry in the placing of characters on the stage, and in the balancing of acts and scenes, monologues and duologues. Its diction too, is limited to a small range of carefully chosen, "noble" words. Goethe's vocabulary further recalls Pietism in its stress on purity, quiet, and the soul; and equally Winckelmann's belief that the Greeks were noble, calm, great-souled, and beautiful. Iphigenia herself is a Winckelmannian figure— statuesque, normally serene, lacking in color; and even the Taurian king behaves with classic dignity. Occasionally, at moments of stress like the "Song of the Fates," the drama shifts from harmonious blank verse to shorter lines.

In later years, Goethe wrote skeptically about the play: if he had known much about the Greeks in younger days, he could never have written *Iphigenia*. Schiller called the drama "amazingly modern and un-Greek"; Goethe admitted that it was "confoundedly humane." Still later, however, he expressed chagrin that the public had treated his "classical" plays coolly; with encouragement, he could have written a dozen pieces like *Iphigenia* and *Tasso*. One shares his regret, for while *Iphigenia* is not great drama in the full sense, it is a subtle and beautiful poem.

Torquato Tasso* (1790) is linked to *Iphigenia* in many ways: in style, in its ethos of decorum, its concentration on interior action. Its iambic pentameter is even more musical than its forerunners. Like a second Iphigenia, the Princess Leonore tries to guide and save the poet Tasso, who loves her; but in this context no healing is possible: the noble lady is herself melancholy and labile. Just below the polished surface of the drama lie madness and despair.

As the play opens—it is set in a country seat of the Duke of Ferrara—Tasso presents the first draft of his masterpiece, *Jerusalem Delivered*, to his patron Duke Alphonso. (It has been well observed that the completion of the poem is no mere episode, but central to the play: a new motif in literature.) The Duke's sister, the Princess, crowns him with a laurel wreath. Antonio, the trusted counselor of the Duke, untimely arrived on the scene, becomes envious, and the Princess' well-meant efforts to reconcile the two lead only to a quarrel; Tasso draws his sword within the ducal palace—theoretically a mortal offense—but the kindly ruler merely confines him to his room. Despite the mildness of the punishment, the poet, whose pathological state becomes increasingly evident, is convinced that everyone, even the Princess, is plotting against him; that the Duke wishes to rob him of his poem.

* Since *Tasso* was begun in Weimar and owes much to Goethe's early experiences there, it is convenient to discuss the play at this point, though it was completed quite a bit later.

RESOLUTION AND FIRST MATURITY

Yet when the Princess assures him of her affection, he takes it as an expression of passion and embraces her. This completes his ruin, at least to his own mind; the Princess and the Duke depart, and Antonio, whose basic decency has gradually become clear, undertakes to comfort the poet. Symbolically, the two men clasp hands; and the last lines of the play contain Tasso's famous and ambiguous image—to which we must return—of the shipwrecked sailor clinging to the rock "on which he was to crash."

So much for the bare (and scanty) bones of the plot. It is easy to dismiss *Tasso* as a drama in which nothing really happens; some have even regarded it as evidence of Goethe's aristocratic bias against a poor distraught poet whose only offenses are to draw his sword when he feels insulted and to embrace a woman who, he thinks, loves him. These actions, however, symbolize Tasso's inability to live in society, within "the law"; they are not mere breaches of etiquette. In any case, the power and significance of *Tasso* lie in its poetry, in its sensitive treatment of the relations among its few but complex characters, and in its presentation of Tasso as an artist.

Tasso's great danger lies in his subjectivity, his inwardness. "His eye barely lingers on this earth," we are told, early in the play. Yet his introversion is not of the arrogant sort; he is diffident about himself and his poetry, and can speak with great charm and insight. All too often, however, he reads his own hopes and fears into others' words; there is a great deal of "talking past the other person" in the drama. At times his suspicions are paranoiac; at others, especially toward the end of the action, he loses all touch with the world around him. He is of course no mere neurotic; if we feel at some points that he is close to insanity, we also have a sense that in a differently constituted group, things might have developed less cruelly for him.

The others bear part of the blame. Successful in practical affairs, Antonio is a frustrated poet; his situation is the reverse of Tasso's. (When Leonore, the confidante of the Princess, remarks that the two must be enemies because nature neglected to make one man of them, we have perhaps a hint that they mirror two aspects of the poet-statesman Goethe.) At any rate, stabler men than Tasso would have been angered by Antonio's rudeness. While the others treat Tasso kindly, they are always trying to guide him, and continually give him moral advice. The theme of education in *Tasso* has been much stressed; each of the three major characters must learn to renounce. In Tasso's case, the education is frustrated, and indeed a dark pall of frustration lies over the play.

Much of this sense of defeat emanates from the character of the Princess, who has her share of what Goethe liked to call "guiltless guilt." Genuinely noble, devoted to Tasso, melancholy and in poor health, she does love him in her "Platonic," rather pallid way. When she tells him, in the fifth act, "My heart cannot forsake you," she is partially responsible for the fatal explosion of his passion. An earlier scene is highly revealing: Tasso has ended a lovely idyllic speech about the Golden Age with the words "What's pleasing is allowed." They do not connote any licentiousness, rather the Renaissance ideal of aristocratic freedom, as symbolized in Rabelais' Abbey of

RESOLUTION AND FIRST MATURITY

Theleme, for example. Yet they are too free for the Princess, who at once revises them to: "What's proper is allowed."

E. M. Wilkinson showed keen insight in giving an essay on *Tasso* the subtitle "The Tragedy of a Creative Artist." He is *an*, not *the* artist; Goethe showed in his Prometheus a "maker" of a very different sort. And while Goethe depicted Tasso with the greatest sympathy—Miss Wilkinson notes "the relentless but compassionate insight, the loving irony"—his attitude is utterly different from romantic glorification of "the poet" or from Thomas Mann's point of view in *Tonio Kröger*. Antonio is neither a villain nor a dull bourgeois; while he behaves badly during the first part of the play, he redeems himself later on. Goethe's statement that his drama showed "the disproportion between talent and life" reflects his sovereign objectivity.

A fatal defect of most poetic treatments of the poet is that we only hear about the protagonist's genius; it is not demonstrated. In *Tasso*, we experience it: passages like the lines on the Golden Age, Tasso's desperate plan to go, disguised as a pilgrim, to visit his sister, and above all the final metaphor of the shipwreck, are completely convincing. Nowhere is Tasso more moving than in his response to the Duke's advice that he live more sanely and cautiously:

> Verbiete du dem Seidenwurm, zu spinnen,
> Wenn er sich schon dem Tode näher spinnt:
> Das köstliche Geweb entwickelt er
> Aus seinem Innersten, und lässt nicht ab,
> Bis er in seinen Sarg sich eingeschlossen.

O geb ein guter Gott uns auch dereinst,
Das Schicksal des beneidenswerten Wurms,
Im neuen Sonnental die Flügel rasch
Und freudig zu entfalten!

Do you forbid the silkworm still to spin,
Because he spins himself more near to death?
The costly web from out his inmost core
He ceaselessly unfolds; and does not pause,
Until he wraps himself within his bier.
Oh! would some friendly god but give us once
The worm's all-enviable destiny—
In some new sunny valley to spread wide
Our wings in joyous rapture!

In the metaphor of the "enviable worm" which will be reborn as a butterfly, Goethe has lent his protagonist his own favorite image of metamorphosis.

There has been much controversy about Goethe's intention in *Tasso*, focused mainly on the interpretation of the play's ending. To Eckermann he stated flatly that the drama was not written to illustrate an "idea"; he had drawn on Tasso's life and his own in conceiving the figure of the poet, and on the courts of Weimar and Ferrara for other matters. In calling the play an intensified or heightened ("gesteigerten") *Werther*, he presumably meant that the whole situation is more highly developed, hence more tense; under such pressures, one infers, Tasso's sufferings are crueler than Werther's, all the more so since his gifts are vastly greater. Turning to the last scene, we find that Tasso finds his own life a ruin—"I am nothing"—but that

RESOLUTION AND FIRST MATURITY

his poetic power remains, though he feels for the moment that he is not sure whether he can ever control it again. Typically, he misunderstands Antonio's admonition to realize his true value by comparing himself with others; he replies that he can think of no one in all history who has suffered more than he. Still, he finds a certain wry consolation in the thought that "If men are silent in their pain / A god gave me to say how much I suffer." In the shipwreck passage, Antonio is the mighty rock; Tasso is at first the wave in which the sun and stars were mirrored. Then suddenly he is the sailor—the sinking ship, with rudder broken, is presumably an image of the course of his life. The rock is his only hope:

> Thus finally the sailor yet clings fast
> Onto the rock, on which he was to crash.

And the play ends. The last line is somewhat ambiguous —was the sailor "fated" to crash or only "expected" to?— in any case, his situation is desperate. It is futile to speculate on Tasso's future, and in a sense the final image forbids us to do so. We know that he has lost all hope of personal happiness, but that he may *perhaps* be able further to express his sufferings in poetry. Thus the ending presents us with "a durative form of the tragic"; Tasso will live on, and his life will continue to be tragic.

Probably the highest achievement of Goethe's first years in Weimar is his lyric poetry. Many of these poems were inspired by Charlotte von Stein; some address her directly. In line with the sense of sublimation, the ideals of discipline, self-restraint, and decorum she evoked in him, the "Charlotte" lyrics deliberately avoid the robust vigor of earlier days and keep their energy under strict control. In "Dedication," which Goethe later put at the head of his collected poems, the Muse is an Iphigenian, divine figure: she heals the "I" of the poem, instructs him, and gently admonishes him. He is no superman:

> By how much do you differ from others?
> Get to know yourself; live at peace with the world!

Having forsworn his youthful arrogance, the poet now finds himself "almost alone" but will try to "show the way" to his brothers. The Muse gives him "the veil* of poetry, woven of morning mist and sunlight clarity, from the hand of truth." The new ideal is an expression of life in which all garish color is classically muted and veiled. In its regular *ottava rima* stanzas the poem exemplifies the "sweet new style," as it has been called, of Goethe's Charlottean mood. "To the Moon" is perhaps the most successful of all these lyrics. After presenting a night scene—a lonely figure, a rushing stream suggesting the "changes of things," the soft light of the moon—the poem closes on the note of withdrawal from the harsh light of day into an inwardness free of bitterness or violent emotion.

> Selig, wer sich vor der Welt
> Ohne Hass verschliesst,
> Einen Freund am Busen hält
> Und mit dem geniesst,

---

* The veil symbol significantly recurs near the end of the "Helen Act" in *Faust II;* see below, p. 209.

RESOLUTION AND FIRST MATURITY

> Was, von Menschen nicht gewusst
> Oder nicht bedacht,
> Durch das Labryrinth der Brust
> Wandelt in der Nacht.

> Happy the man who shuts himself off from the world without hatred, keeps a friend close to his heart and enjoys with him
> what, unknown by men, or unconsidered, moves at night through the labyrinth of the breast.

In only one poem of this period, "The Chalice," is the mood of sublimation or resignation broken; here the otherworldly veil has been lifted: the imagery is strikingly erotic.

A number of poems express Goethe's new ethical orientation, which derives largely from Spinoza, but with the philosopher's pantheism in part counteracted by the dualistic view of Frau von Stein. While Goethe generally saw God and nature—*Deus sive natura*—as the two aspects of the same basic reality, he wrote in "The Divine" that nature was unfeeling and amoral; like Emerson, he now held that "law for man" and "law for thing" were utterly different:

> For man alone can
> Perform the impossible:
> He can distinguish,
> Choose and give judgment;
> He can impart to the
> Moment duration.

Generally, however, Goethe remains Spinozistic. Man can win "human freedom" only by overcoming himself. He must keep free of self-destructive remorse and hatred, as "To the Moon" reminds us. Intellectually he knows that the divinity cannot be judged anthropomorphically, but that it is almost inevitable to revere the immortals:

> As if they were men, and
> Did on the grand scale,
> What the best man in little
> Does, or would like to.

In *Wilhelm Meister's Apprenticeship* the poet secularized Spinoza's sublime statement that the man who truly loves God cannot ask that God love him in return. The actress Philina, an attractive if somewhat promiscuous little thing, remarks to the hero: "If I love you, what business is it of yours?"

The lovely poem "Song of the Spirits over the Waters" has the relation between fate and the soul as its theme. Evoked by a Swiss waterfall, it symbolizes the eternal cycle of the soul, descending from heaven, then rising again from the earth, in the element of water. Its course is not predetermined in detail: as the water makes its long descent over the cliff, the wind intervenes; it is blown this way and that by the wind; its flow may be headlong or placid:

> Soul of a mortal,
> How like to the water!
> Fate of a mortal,
> How like to the wind!

RESOLUTION AND FIRST MATURITY

It is tempting to see in the very shape of the poem on the printed page an image of the slender waterfall, but the resemblance is probably a coincidence; Goethe used this form, with its short lines, for a variety of themes.

Two longer poems testify to Goethe's basically ethical approach in these days. "Harz Journey in the Winter" is still written with Storm-and-Stress boldness and fire, in free verse. "Let my song soar like the hawk . . . ," it begins. Alone, the poet sets out into the wild mountain country, partly perhaps for the sake of sheer adventure, primarily to try to help an outcast, a misanthrope. This unfortunate, "first despised, now a despiser," is consuming himself in futile resentments. Aware of the "fullness of love" which permeates the world, the poet begs the "Father of love" to open the eyes of the unhappy man to the "thousand fountains" which could quench his thirst in this self-imposed desert. (In imagery as well as in its ethos, this section of the poem recalls "Mohammed's Song.") We never learn the outcome of the venture. Indeed, there is something fragmentary and erratic about "Harz Journey," but it conveys a sense of altruistic love which was magnificently translated into music by Brahms.

A second highly "confessional" poem, "Ilmenau," was dedicated to Karl August on the Duke's twenty-sixth birthday. The poem takes its name from the small town near Weimar which Goethe had saved from economic ruin by restoring its silver mines; thus the title of this invocation of social responsibility and maturity is an appropriate one. By a bold use of the *Doppelgänger* motif —the poet appears in two different figures, his former and his present self—Goethe contrasts past and present, wild youth and anxious manhood, the carefree life of the court and the misery of the poor. His mood is one of self-reproach: "I brought pure fire from the altar, / The fire I kindled is no pure flame." Criticizing himself with undue harshness, he is able to deliver, with good grace, a fairly severe admonition to the Duke. (Goethe, as these verses prove, was anything but a sychophant.) When the poet apologizes for indiscreet praise of unconstrained freedom (presumably with reference to *Götz* and perhaps to poems like "Prometheus") one feels that he has become all too well adjusted to the world of the Weimar court. Yet a charming sense of humor saves "Ilmenau" from the danger of undue conformity.

Among the many other poems of the time, at least a few must be mentioned. Not without reason, the two "Wanderer's Night Songs" are often thought to be Goethe's supreme lyrical achievements. The first was dedicated to Charlotte:

> Der du von dem Himmel bist,
> Alles Leid und Schmerzen stillest,
> Den, der doppelt elend ist,
> Doppelt mit Erquickung füllest,
> Ach, ich bin des Treibens müde!
> Was soll all der Schmerz und Lust?
> Süsser Friede,
> Komm, ach komm in meine Brust!

*

> Über allen Gipfeln
> Ist Ruh,

RESOLUTION AND FIRST MATURITY

> In allen Wipfeln
> Spürest du
> Kaum einen Hauch;
> Die Vögelein schweigen im Walde.
> Warte nur, balde
> Ruhest du auch.

Both are quoted in the English of Longfellow, a mediocre poet, but a splendid translator:

> Thou that from the heavens art,
> Every pain and sorrow stillest,
> And the doubly wretched heart
> Doubly with refreshment fillest,
> I am weary with contending!
> Why this rapture and unrest?
> Peace descending
> Come, ah, come into my breast!

*

> O'er all the hill-tops
> Is quiet now,
> In all the tree-tops
> Hearest thou
> Hardly a breath;
> The birds are asleep in the trees:
> Wait; soon like these
> Thou too shalt rest.

Alcman's lyric of the seventh century B.C. affords both a parallel and a contrast to Goethe's second "Night Song":

> Asleep lie mountain-top and mountain-gully, shoulder also and ravine; the creeping things that come from the dark earth, the beasts whose lying is upon the hillside, the generation of the bees, the monsters in the depths of the purple brine, all lie asleep, and with them the tribes of the winged birds.

In contrast to this completely objective "landscape," Goethe's poem, progressing from the inorganic through the animal world to man, ends by implying the subjective emotion of the human being: "Thou too shalt rest." This has often been felt as particularly "modern." But one should not try to derive any grandiose historical contrast from this; Alcman's lyric is preserved only on a partially destroyed page: he may have had more to say.

One other poem should be mentioned, the most famous if not the greatest of Goethe's ballads, "The Erl King." Prosaic reality and the supernatural— the sick child's vision of the king of the elves and his daughters—are juxtaposed dramatically. Rarely has man's ancient fear of the dark been more concisely conveyed: the first line—"Who rides so late through night and wind?"—appeals to a stratum of atavistic terror, and the daemonic effect is heightened by the passion of the uncanny king for the dying boy.

Thus the poetic yield of the first eleven years in Weimar was both varied and great. It must however have been disappointing to Goethe: too many great plans remained unfinished. Public affairs became burdensome. After all, once the poet had proved his practical ability, *cui bono?* Doubtless the Duke could find dozens of capable administrators; there was only one man who could finish *Tasso* and *Wilhelm Meister,* and he was kept "too busy."

This absurd situation was made the more painful by

RESOLUTION AND FIRST MATURITY

the poet's frustrated desire, felt since boyhood, to go to Italy. ("Italy" can be used as shorthand for the whole sphere of the Mediterranean South, classical beauty, Rome as city and symbol, and the freedom, as artist and man, to live for one's authentic needs.) So poignant had Goethe's longing for "the land, where the lemon-blossoms flower" (see page 87) become that he was no longer able, he wrote later, to read a book written in Latin; it was emotionally unbearable.

To leave, obviously, would be a repudiation of Charlotte and all she stood for. Undoubtedly, she had been his solace; equally clearly, he now again felt the need to escape. She had given him, for years, a sense of stability and purpose, but the price was becoming too great. A "repeated puberty" was becoming manifest; soon Goethe would incur the "guiltless guilt" of metamorphosis, of becoming a different person.

In these years, the study of science had been another consolation; it would continue to be a major interest throughout his life. When Goethe discovered* the intermaxillary bone in man, his joy was at least as great as if he had triumphantly finished a major poem. "I have found, not gold or silver, but something which makes me much happier . . ." he proclaimed, in a letter to Herder. The existence of this bone (part of the upper jaw) in man had long been denied, though everyone knew that it existed in the apes. Thus man was, anatomically at least, an integral part of the great chain of nature; the sharp divi-

---

* Or rediscovered: Vicq d'Azyr apparently made the find a bit earlier, but Goethe worked quite independently.

sion between a man and the rest of creation, asserted in Goethe's very uncharacteristic poem "The Divine," could no longer be maintained. Rudolf Magnus holds that the poet proved himself, by this discovery, one of the great founders of comparative anatomy. Academic scientists stubbornly rejected Goethe's finding: what he had seen did not conform to accepted dogma. The same thing happened again when he published his anti-Newtonian *Theory of Colors*. His dislike of professors was not ill-founded.

During the Italian journey to come, Goethe was to find the discovery of the "archetypal plant" (as he thought it) as important as Raphael's paintings, or the temples at Paestum, or reading the Odyssey. Barker Fairley has remarked that Goethe never divorced his study of the classical world from that of nature. Here was another factor which tended to estrange him from Charlotte. A dualist, introspective, she could not share his belief in "God-nature." He immersed himself in anatomy, meteorology, geology; she found rocks "nasty."

For a variety of reasons, Goethe's whole view of life was changing; no single factor can account for the inner revolution which was taking place in him. His sense of malaise gradually became critical. Too much altruism, discipline, devotion to the "demands of the day"—and too much "Platonic" love?—threatened to alienate him from his real self. In September, 1786, he left for Rome, telling no one of his goal. It was a flight, but Goethe's real aim was freedom *for* something, even more than liberation *from* something; it was self-realization.

4. TOWARD A NEW CLASSICISM

MANY YEARS BEFORE HIS ITALIAN JOURNEY, IN HIS STORM-and-Stress days, Goethe had visited the famous Hall of Antiquities in Mannheim, a collection of reproductions of Greek and Hellenistic statues, including the Apollo Belvedere and the Laocoön. He wrote, in *Poetry and Truth*, of the "irresistible" effect which this "forest of statues" had made on him. Yet this early encounter, he added, had only slight consequences for the time being: "hardly had the door of the splendid hall closed behind me, when I wished to find myself again; indeed I rather tried to banish those figures from my imagination, as a burden; and I was to be guided back into their circle only by a very roundabout path."

These words were written long after the event, and it may be that Goethe transformed literal "truth" into "poetry," in this instance as in others; but they are symbolically true at all events. The "roundabout path" which finally took him to Rome did in fact lead him into the circle of pagan gods and classical art.

Inevitably, Goethe's Greeks were seen through the eyes of his own time; more precisely, through those of Winckelmann, "the first great aesthetic educator of the Germans." We no longer equate Rome with Greece; we find the Apollo Belvedere late and the Laocoön more baroque than classical. The Greece of Winckelmann and Goethe was a myth, a world of pure forms, marble whiteness, "noble simplicity and quiet grandeur" in ethical as well as aesthetic matters. This "classical" Greece, Santayana noted, was "the most romantic thing in the history of mankind." Yet the myth was a highly stimulating and productive one; in that sense, there was truth in it. And Goethe was finally, like Faust, to progress through and beyond it.

Goethe made all possible speed on his way to Rome; not even Florence could detain him. While he was attracted by certain Renaissance painters, he had lost his early enthusiasm for the Gothic: simple, monumental proportions now seemed the ideal. Significantly, of the moderns it was Raphael—the greatest "imitator" of Greek art, according to Winckelmann—and the classical Palladio whom he most admired. But like Winckelmann before him, he believed that only in Rome would he discover the true essence of beauty.

It was not a matter of art alone. Like so many Northerners before and after him, Goethe believed that only in the South could he find happy, healthy, "whole" people. In his mind, Germany was more and more associated with gloom, cold, and deprivation. While the German was alienated from himself, fragmented as it were, the Italian was "solid," sensuous, and somehow, whatever his faults,

TOWARD A NEW CLASSICISM

a complete man. ". . . I've gotten to know happy people, who are that only because they are whole; even the humblest if he is whole can be happy and in his way perfect," he reported to Herder. Searching for completeness of this sort, he lived incognito as "Filippo Miller [or Möller], German painter," associating mainly with artists. He thus escaped from the ceremony and decorum of Weimar life and hoped also to avoid curious tourists—as the author of *Werther*, he was a European celebrity—and visiting dignitaries.

In Italy Goethe gradually gained the intuition that the works of nature and those of classic art follow the same inherent principles. "Everything arbitrary, merely imagined falls away; there is necessity, there is God." Just as the concrete "archetypal plant" contains in itself the basic form of all plants, Greek sculpture holds fast the eternal archetypes of man. Art does not imitate nature, but is coordinate with it. Ethics must harmonize with aesthetics; the true *is* the beautiful. Homer's figures are "solid," unsurpassable; they are "natural," not in any romantic sense but as exemplars of eternal types. In his travels through Sicily, in 1787, Goethe believed that he had found the "archetypal landscape" of the Homeric world. Taking a theme from the *Odyssey*, he attempted to write an authentic classical tragedy, "Nausicaä," but abandoned the attempt as impossible.

This new orientation—Goethe's second classicism, as it were—meant of course a sharp break with the world of Weimar idealism. It now became obvious to him that the Greeks of his *Iphigenia in Tauris* were modern, humane, half-Christian. Breaking with the Platonism—in both senses—of Charlotte's sphere, Goethe emphasized the here-and-now, the eternal in the present, the "this-worldly." For a time, the pagan strain in his nature was far stronger than the Christian. Thus he noted in the *Italian Journey* that many people in the modern era needed to be given false consolation "and therefore so many churches were built," while the ancients could face reality. Despite this and many similar statements, a Northern, reflective, more or less Christian element still persisted in Goethe: after all, he finished the revision of *Iphigenia* in Italy, virtually completed *Tasso*, and wrote an extremely Gothic scene of *Faust* there—the "Witch's Kitchen." But at least in his conscious mind paganism predominated. In art as in life the goal is the "true, existent" realized form, the *Gestalt*. Such figures are not subject to courtly etiquette or Christian morality.

The *Roman Elegies** present timeless archetypal figures—primarily a lover and his mistress—in the medium of poetry. Thus while the girl celebrated in the *Elegies* is convincingly real, she is not individualized in the manner of a Lotte or an Iphigenia; she is *a* beautiful, warm-blooded, rather earthy woman. With his new emphasis on the wholeness of all life, Goethe compares her growth to that of a vine-blossom which has ripened into a grape. The lovers are very much of this world, with something of the three-dimensionality of statues, but with no marmoreal coldness. Their love, as part of the natural order

---

* They were not published until 1795, and much of the content was drawn from post-Roman experiences, but in essence they are Roman indeed.

TOWARD A NEW CLASSICISM

of things, is seen as holy. Unrequited love is a slow poison, for

> In the heroical age, when gods were goddesses' lovers,
> Appetite came from one glance, pleasure came hard on desire.

While the "I" of the *Elegies* is somewhat more individualized than the girl—the lover who speaks is also a self-conscious German poet—these poems are part of a European literary tradition and by no means wholly "confessional." In this series of twenty poems in classical distichs, Goethe was deliberately following Tibullus, Propertius, and Ovid. From them he took various stock themes: the need of secrecy in love, the tricked guardian, the appeals to Venus.

One passage in particular, which has shocked or amused many readers, probably owes at least as much to Propertius as to immediate experience. In the Fifth Elegy, after telling how the touch of his beloved's body has given him his first understanding of sculpture, the poet tells of gently counting out the measure of his hexameters on the back of his sleeping mistress. The Roman elegist had similarly written of reading his poems aloud while in the embrace of his Cynthia, a "learned maid." Goethe's *Elegies* combine "lived experience" with cultural experience, tradition with the individual talent.

While the Latin elegy was marked by a certain frivolity, Goethe makes occasional use of irony and varies between lightness and seriousness. His Fourth Elegy proclaims that lovers are "pious," but the poet uses the word in the Roman sense of devotion to the cults of all the gods, and invokes an unfamiliar god, Occasion, for their amorous purposes. A German in Rome, he adopts for the moment the classical point of view and calls himself a barbarian.

In writing about sexual love with "antique frankness," Goethe was defying, or at any rate criticizing, his own time. Even Herder advised against publishing the *Elegies,* and when they did appear, the Weimarians were duly shocked. Four, including two poems devoted to Priapus, were long suppressed. It is revealing that various Weimar ladies referred to the poet himself by that name, when he returned from Rome after an absence of almost two years. However excessive, even hysterical their reaction was, it was not completely senseless: the *Elegies* do point, both by precept and example, toward a pagan style of life. "Live a happy life," Amor tells the poet in the Thirteenth Elegy, "and let antiquity live again within you!" He calls the advice sophistical, but follows it nevertheless.

When he left Rome for the North, Goethe felt like Ovid at the time of his banishment. Some three years later he was back in Italy; the *Venetian Epigrams*,[*] set like the *Elegies* in classical distichs, are often compared with them. Yet the mood of the *Epigrams* is an utterly different one: harsh, uncharacteristically bitter, at times (especially in the verses long withheld from publication) savagely obscene. Of course, the poet was writing in a different genre: Martial and the *Priapea* were now his models; but why were just these models chosen?

[*] Mainly written in 1790; published 1795.

TOWARD A NEW CLASSICISM

The major answers lie in Goethe's private life and in the course of political events. Back in Weimar, he found himself almost completely alienated from his old friends; they thought him cold, self-absorbed, sensuous; and his constant expressions of longing for Italy injured their local pride. On his return, as if to demonstrate his new pagan ethic, he took a young factory girl, Christiane Vulpius, into his home. She seems to have been attractive, good-natured, and—to judge by letters which still exist—completely uneducated and uninterested in literature. With refreshing directness and no overtone of disapproval, Goethe's mother referred to Christiane as his "bed-treasure." Naturally, this liaison made the break with Charlotte von Stein far more drastic. Weimar society would have no doubt forgiven any number of affairs, but a permanent *mésalliance* was something else: "Mamselle Vulpius" was ostracized. When Goethe had to go to Venice in the spring of 1790—it was a courtesy to the Duke, whose mother planned to spend some time there—he bitterly missed Christiane and their infant son.* This tended to put him into a very surly mood; he had already been depressed by the outbreak of the French Revolution the year before. Nasty weather in Venice, and the alleged dishonesty of Italian inn-keepers and servants also did their part.

The *Venetian Epigrams* begin boldly, on a Dionysiac note: the Ancients adorned their sarcophagi and urns with fauns and Bacchantes; these verses should also be

---

* August, born 1789, was the only child of this union to survive infancy. Goethe did not legally marry Christiane until 1806; she died in 1816.

testimonials of life. But the third short poem strikes the note of homesickness; the fourth states flatly: "This is no longer the Italy that I left with sorrow." The poet is disillusioned with ordinary people—"Works of the mind and of art do not exist for the mob"—and with the rulers and "good society" as well. He has even begun to have his doubts about Italy as the shrine of ancient art. Not only religious pilgrims deceive themselves: "We are all pilgrims, we who seek Italy/—It is only scattered bones we revere, with happy credulity." The anti-Christian mood reaches a climax in the lines declaring that there are four things which the normally patient traveller hates: "tobacco smoke, lice, and garlic and the Cross." Although the "lyrical I" repeatedly speaks of his longing for his wife and child, there are hints of passion for a young girl (an acrobat) and of adventures with ordinary prostitutes. Some of the suppressed epigrams are downright clinical in their approach to religious hysteria and sexual perversion. Two or three positive poems, like the graceful tribute to his Maecenas, Duke Karl August, appear like Vergil's shipwrecked sailors, swimming in the vast whirlpool. Like many works of very different temper, the *Venetian Epigrams* seems to have afforded Goethe a catharsis; here he rid himself of black bile.

Throughout the 1790's, Goethe was deeply concerned with the attempt to understand the French Revolution. At first he tried to dismiss it as the product of corruption and demagoguery. A series of comedies, some of them fragmentary, attempt to explain, and to ridicule, the Revolution in these terms; it is no wonder that these dramas have been virtually forgotten. (Actually, he knew better himself: after witnessing the check administered to the Prussian army by the French at Valmy, in 1792, he remarked that a new epoch of world history had begun then and there.) The satire *Reynard the Fox* and various epigrammatic verses of the decade reflect his dismay and disgust, as well as his aversion to those Germans who sympathized with the new movement. Only in his "domestic epic," *Hermann and Dorothea*,* did he admit the nobility of the idealistic supporters of the Revolution. At the end of the decade he began work on a tragedy in blank verse, *The Natural Daughter*. Finished in 1803, it was intended as the first part of a trilogy. To some extent, Goethe's failure to carry out this plan may have been caused by the cool reception given *The Natural Daughter*, but there are intrinsic reasons as well.

Unfortunately, the drama has become associated with two very damaging comments: the formula "marble-smooth and marble-cold" and Herder's characteristically tactless remark to Goethe: "I prefer your natural son"—meaning poor August, of course. Actually, the tragedy is by no means cold. The character of the daughter Eugenia—proud, beautiful, impetuous—is splendidly realized, as is her father's grief when he thinks her dead. In fact, the raw material of the drama is sensational, far more "exciting" than Goethe's plots usually are. The action, based on the *Mémoires* of Stéphanie de Bourbon-Conti, tells of the intrigue of jealous relatives to kidnap the natural daughter of a duke in order to prevent her legit-

---

* See below, pp. 96 f.

imization, and to deport her to a sinister tropical island after giving out the report of her death.

Goethe took great care to establish "aesthetic distance" by treating the matter abstractly. In this he was only too successful. Everything takes place in the curious, half-real world of a decadent *ancien régime*. No places or times are identified; only Eugenia—"the wellborn"—has a name; the main villain never appears on the stage. While there are striking symbolic actions, like Eugenia's fall during a hunt, presaging a greater fall to come, we are left in doubt about her final fate and that of the state. The action ends with a question mark, as it were. For the sake of giving the aesthetic semblance of events rather than crude reality, Goethe greatly diminished the tragic force of the play. With its many abstract nouns and sententious generalizations, the stylized language is often manneristic and does indeed seem "marble-cold" to many readers. It is however often of a symmetrical, very formal beauty, as in the following exchange:

> EUGENIA: My fortune, friend, is firm beyond recall.
> COMPANION: Beyond recall the fate that strikes you down.

The "happy event," as Goethe called it, which offset the troubles of the 1790's and may well have saved him from isolation and sterility, was the establishment of his friendship with Schiller. At first their relation was cool, even hostile: Schiller, ten years younger, still struggling against poverty, naturally envied the established poet. For his part, Goethe distrusted Schiller as the wild au-

TOWARD A NEW CLASSICISM

thor of *The Robbers* and, as such, a painful reminder of his own Storm-and-Stress days; he did not realize that Schiller had outgrown that drama just as he himself had long since grown away from the sphere of *Götz von Berlichingen*. Thanks to Schiller's initiative and tact, a *rapprochement* was established. After a conversation with Goethe on scientific matters, which must have been more lively than cordial, Schiller composed his amazing letter of August 23, 1794; it is actually a miniature essay, and one of the most important documents of German literature. After contrasting his own speculative, abstract mode of thought to Goethe's power of intuitive observation, he went on:

> If you had been born as a Greek, yes even as an Italian, and if a choice nature and an idealizing art had been your surroundings from birth, your path [toward attaining a classical style] would have been infinitely shortened, would perhaps have been rendered quite unnecessary. . . . Now, since you were born a German, since your Greek spirit was hurled into this Northern world, you had no other choice than either to become a Northern artist yourself or by substituting in your imagination, through the power of thought, the element of which reality had deprived it; and thus intellectually, as it were, giving birth to a Greece of your own from within.

Nothing could have pleased Goethe more; his correspondent had indeed sensed the problem of writing objective, classical poetry in an unclassical time and place. Near the end of the letter, Schiller expressed the hope their two minds, the one speculative, the other intuitive,* would

* The two types correspond to Schiller's famous contrast between the "sentimentive" and the "naive."

"meet each other halfway." Just this took place: in his reply, Goethe thanked Schiller for "casting the sum of my existence with a friendly hand." Each was to find the other's criticism enormously stimulating. Without Schiller's prodding, Goethe would have finished *Meister's Apprenticeship* and *Faust,* Part I, later, if at all. And there were lesser products also: the jointly written *Xenia,* the friendly competition of the "Ballad Year," and collaboration in matters of aesthetic and dramatic theory. It was not an emotional friendship; the two never used the intimate "Du" to each other, and there were inevitable frictions. Occasionally Goethe feared that Schiller's philosophical, highly analytic mind would injure his poetic talent by making him too self-conscious. For his part, Schiller seems to have been hurt at times by a certain reserve in the older man. But the bond was a literary and personal alliance, faithfully maintained by both poets until Schiller's death in 1805. At its best, it was a marriage of true minds. When Goethe was asked, years later, which of the *Xenia* had been written by him, which by Schiller, he replied that he was no longer sure: in some instances, one had the idea, the other wrote the epigram; or one would write the hexameter (of a given distich) and the other would supply the pentameter.

Encouraged by Schiller, who read the several sections of the long novel as Goethe finished them, he finally completed *Wilhelm Meister's Apprenticeship;* the book was published in 1795–96. Taking up the project again after a break of some ten years confronted Goethe with a difficult task: he felt differently now about the theater, about the relative importance of literature and practical life, about various social classes and types of character. In short, he had become a different person; to play an active part in the real world now appeared more significant to him than any "theatrical mission." As Novalis observed, poetry is defeated in *Meister:* Wilhelm abandons the stage; Mignon, the embodiment, among other things, of lyrical longing, dies. There is a sharp break in the novel: the first five sections or books correspond roughly to the old torso; the sixth plunges us suddenly into the introverted world of German Pietism; the last two are devoted to getting Wilhelm away from the theater, instructing him in the meaning of life ("Remember to live"), tying up all the threads of the plot, often rather hastily, and rewarding the hero with the promise of a happy marriage. The idea of gradually developing the cultivation of mind and character (*Bildung*), remains central, but the direction of the process changes. At first, one's interest largely centers on the growth of Wilhelm's abilities and tastes as an actor, student of the theater, and potential poet. As already noted, the theater itself appears in all the metamorphoses of its development, from the puppet show to Shakespeare. (The hero's name is significant: "Wilhelm" is a tribute to Shakespeare; "Meister" is largely ironic, for he well realizes himself how far he is from any mastery.) Largely, his *Bildung* depends on a galaxy of women: among others the actress Mariana, the fascinating Philina, Mignon, and finally Natalia, the almost too ideal character whose hand he wins at the end. Simultaneously, he is growing away from the rather stuffy middle-class atmosphere of his family—like Thomas Mann's protagonists, he is "de-burgherized"—and then from the Bohemian milieu of the actors; he marries into the aristocracy. Up to that point, his life has been largely made up of illusions and errors. Wrongly believing his first love unfaithful, he leaves her with unconscious cruelty; he is clay in the hands of unscrupulous actors and later of the "Society of the Tower," a group of well-meaning gentlemen who direct his apprenticeship in the latter course of the novel. His whole theatrical career is founded on the mistaken notion that he is a born actor; actually, he is a dilettante who can play only one sort of role successfully: "Hamlet types" like himself. Thus he abandons the stage, just as Goethe himself had renounced the hope of becoming a painter. On the last page of the book, he is compared to Saul the son of Kish, who went out to seek his father's she-asses, and found a kingdom. This insight into himself, into the ironic contrast between hopes and realization, aims and results, is winning; and it is typical of Wilhelm. He never loses his charm, his interest in life and ideas. Unlike Faust, to whom he has often been compared and contrasted, he is genuinely kind, befriending a succession of outcasts. If he is naive—one sharp-tongued woman character compares him to a bird-of-paradise who never can find a perch—he does learn, like his twentieth-century descendant, Hans Castorp. In line with Goethe's theory of the novel, Wilhelm is a passive hero, who rarely acts independently, but he is never negligible. The poet's ambivalence toward Meister comes out in his letters, where Wilhelm is described at one point as a "poor creature," at another as "my beloved dramatic image." At any rate, he inherited a great deal of the young Goethe's almost irresistible charisma.

TOWARD A NEW CLASSICISM

Much of the appeal of *Meister's Apprenticeship* lies in the enigmatic, magical figure of Mignon. A genuinely symbolic character, she cannot be completely explained: she "stands for" poetry perhaps, for romantic longing, but is too sharply individualized to be reduced to an allegory. Goethe has avoided sentimentality by showing Mignon as a clearly pathological human being; her impulses are strange, her appearance ambiguous. At least at one point in the novel, Mignon is referred to as "he." When she and the old Harper appear in the book, poetry and tragedy are suddenly there; both must disappear before the novel can proceed to its happy ending. Goethe's lyrical genius is at its height in the songs she sings and in some of the Harper's. The most famous of them expresses Mignon's longing for the South, and his own:

> Kennst du das Land, wo die Zitronen blühn,
> Im dunkeln Laub die Gold-Orangen glühn,
> Ein sanfter Wind vom blauen Himmel weht,
> Die Myrte still und hoch der Lorbeer steht,
> Kennst du es wohl?
>   Dahin! Dahin
> Möcht' ich mit dir, o mein Geliebter, ziehn!

Do you know the land, where the lemons flower, / in the dark leaves the golden oranges glow, / a gentle wind blows from the blue sky, / the myrtle stands quiet, and the laurel tall? / Do you indeed know it? / There, there / beloved, I would go with you.

The poem proceeds swiftly to evoke the gleaming classic halls of Italy and then the dangerous journey northward over the Alpine passes, giving us, with the utmost compression, the crucial memories of Mignon's life. Other lyrics, like Philina's characteristic song about the amorous joys of night, enrich the book; they helped to set a fashion of lyrical insertions in the romantic novel.

As Mignon is the emotional high point of the book, the discussions of Shakespeare form its intellectual climax. Wilhelm's analysis of Hamlet's character is brilliant but characteristically subjective. By portraying him as a sensitive, delicate soul, he founded a romantic interpretation of the Prince which still has its defenders:

> ... it is clear to me that Shakespeare wished to describe a great deed imposed upon a soul which is not equal to the deed. ... Here an oak is planted in a costly vessel which should have received only lovely flowers within it; the roots spread outward, the vessel is destroyed.
>
> A beautiful, pure, noble, highly moral being, without the strength of sinew which makes the hero, perishes under a burden that it can neither bury nor cast off. ...

While this presents one aspect of Hamlet's character unforgettably, it ignores the vigorous, ruthless side of the young man who fought with pirates and sent Rosencrantz and Guildenstern to the death they deserved. Wilhelm's Hamlet is a cousin of Werther.

The Society of the Tower, already referred to, is made up of leisured aristocrats devoted largely to furthering the development of its members, and helping to guide promising young men toward *Bildung,* though it has practical aspects as well. While the Society believes in letting its "apprentices" learn through erring, it can nevertheless intervene sharply when its own interests are

TOWARD A NEW CLASSICISM

threatened. Goethe borrowed the device of a mysterious secret society from the popular novel of the day. As the book approaches its end, he uses it increasingly as a piece of epic machinery which enables him to manipulate his characters easily, perhaps all too easily. Emissaries of the "Tower" interfere even with Wilhelm's choice of a wife. If Goethe's attitude toward the Society shows traces of irony—and indeed, on the literal level, it has its absurd side—he still presents it in a generally favorable way. Its members pronounce the didactic message of the novel.

Central to activities of the Society is the "Hall of the Past," dedicated to the motto "Remember to live." Built in a serene classic style, it contains a great number of pictures, each symbolizing an archetypal moment of life:

> Nothing is transitory except the individual who enjoys and watches [the scene of life]. This picture here of the mother pressing her child to her heart will outlive many generations of happy mothers.

Similarly, at the end of Mignon's funeral rites, the chorus insistently repeats the words "Return to life." After paying his tribute to the dead, man must devote his thoughts to "day and happiness and permanence." Schiller congratulated Goethe for having broken sharply with the "accursed *memento mori*," and the "this-worldly," non-Christian emphasis of the novel is evident.

The "letter of instruction" which is read to Wilhelm stresses the variety and richness of human life:

> From the slightest animal attempts at labor to the highest practice of intellectual art, from the babbling and crowing of the infant to the most polished utterance of the orator and the

bard, from the first scuffling of boys to the vast armaments by which countries are conquered and held, from the merest trace of kindly feeling and the most fleeting love to the most violent passion and the most serious union . . . all these and much more are latent in man and must be cultivated; yet not in one individual but in many. Every innate gift (*Anlage*) is important, and it must be developed. . . .

The proper education of man, we may infer, is too broad and complex a matter to be contained within a neat definition. At any rate, the novel refuses to give us one. We believe Wilhelm when he says: ". . . to develop all of myself, just as I am, has been in a dark way my wish and purpose since youth." About a *specific* purpose or goal, Goethe deliberately leaves us largely in the dark.

Not entirely, of course. When Wilhelm willingly assumes responsibility for his son by the actress Mariana, who has since died—he had been long unaware of his existence—the Society takes this as proof that he has reached maturity. In the act of marriage, he will be building a bridge to the actual world. Like the chorus at Mignon's funeral, he is turning toward life. We never see him as a man of action but must take his development to maturity on faith (see pages 121–29).

Readers have felt that *Meister's Apprenticeship* is too heavily didactic, and at the same time not concretely didactic enough; the two criticisms do not really contradict each other. It has been charged that Goethe "ruined" his novel by changing its direction in the middle of its course. To me this seems unduly harsh, but no one is likely to claim that the book is a fully integrated work of art. With his characteristic acumen, Schiller pointed out that the facts of the novel somehow did not quite harmonize with its "idea" or intention, and that the latter should be more clearly presented. While Goethe agreed to make some changes in his manuscript, he refused, with quiet stubbornness, to be as clear as Schiller wanted him to be. Goethe wrote of *Faust* that it was a poem like life itself: "It has indeed a beginning, an end, but it is not a whole." The judgment fits *Meister's Apprenticeship* more closely. Perhaps the notion that the novel, or one standard form of the novel, is like a journey, with many meanderings and digressions, is a helpful one here. Wilhelm's journey was a long one, sometimes exhausting or confusing, but we are richer for having accompanied him.

In "The Fairy Tale" (1795) one is faced with a symbolic story like that of such romantic writers as Novalis. As in Kafka's tales, happenings flow into one another in a dreamlike manner, and Goethe's work is as enigmatic as any of Kafka's. It has been read as a political allegory and as a disguised account of pregnancy and birth, but such simplistic interpretations explain both too little and too much. One cannot reduce true symbols to ordinary prose. A few points however are clear: "The Fairy Tale" does deal with a time (like the 1790's) when one order is dying, another is emerging. "The time has come!" is a repeated motif; birth or rebirth is the theme, or at least a theme, of the tale. A mysterious and beautiful snake sacrifices itself voluntarily. Somehow this is decisive, and the tantalizing tale ends with the triumph of love.

During a few days of June, 1797, Goethe wrote two of his most extraordinary poems, the ballads "The Bride of

Corinth" and "The God and the Bajadere." The former employs the vampire motif—a very strange choice for the poet to select at a time when he believed fervently in the ideals of a serene and decorous classicism. Again he has chosen a time of transition: in this case, that from Greek paganism to Christianity. To his natural dislike of sudden historical changes (he deplored the Reformation as well as the French Revolution) must be added the particular aversion which he felt at this time for the Christian faith as a religion which denied life. This violent rejection of his inherited belief seems to have had its inception in Italy; it was to last for many years, though not until the end of his life. "The Bride of Corinth" tells of a Greek youth who visits the girl to whom he has been engaged from childhood; her family has since become Christian, and he worries about his reception:

> When a new religion is germinating, / love and loyalty are often / rooted up like an evil weed.

She nevertheless comes to his room; they become lovers; but he must die since the girl he embraced is a vampire. Banished to a cell at her mother's command, she had perished, a victim of pious fanaticism. Passion for him has brought her back from the grave, but now their only hope is to join the old gods after death.

"The God and the Bajadere" also tells, though in a less polemical mood, of a supernatural and uncanny love. An Indian temple-prostitute loves the god who comes to her in disguise—a theme reminiscent of *Egmont* and "The New Melusina." After his apparent death, she flings her-

TOWARD A NEW CLASSICISM

self into the flames of his pyre and is raised to heaven in his arms. In both poems, the familiar Goethean theme of dying to be reborn is again sounded.

Throughout these years, Goethe's new "classical" view of the world became more sharply defined and more inclusive. In literature, art, science, and life, the same archetypal patterns appear, aspects of the same integrating law. At times he emphasized the eternal nature of the pattern—"permanence in change"—at others the metamorphoses which continually are taking place—"change within permanence." He perceived for example in his anatomical studies that whereas the bones of a particular animal's skeleton vary widely from those of other species in size and shape, the basic structural pattern remains the same. His is not a rigid classicism; it is a flexible, shifting universe he evokes, but one which moves according to eternal principles. The individual and the principle are equally real.

Perhaps a few examples will show how these generalizations illuminate his poetry. In various elegies of the late 1790's, all concerned with love, the individuals are real, their emotions peculiar to them and very sharply felt. The personages of "Alexis and Dora" and "Amyntas" have Greek names not because they are ideal types, still less allegories, but because the poet believed that in Greek life one found the most beautiful, in a sense the "realest," human beings—concrete universals, as it were. Similarly, in using classical meter during this period, he was choosing that one form out of the countless "metamorphoses" of poetic language which seemed to him most generally valid.* It is quite true that Goethe's poems of this type have less emotional impact than the great poetry written in his native tradition, but what they lose in immediacy, they gain in "distance," which was exactly his intention. "Amyntas" presents the symbol of an apple tree, overgrown by ivy; when the gardener wishes to cut it away, the tree protests: though the vine is draining away its marrow, its very soul, it is bound to the tree by a thousand tendrils; both would die if one did. Amyntas at once applies the metaphor to his own life: though his love is consuming him he cannot renounce it. It is the familiar Goethean theme of the ill-matched lovers. He must often have felt encumbered and dragged down by Christiane, but he has shown that a very keenly felt personal experience is typical and thus in his sense classical. Perhaps the tension between the personal emotion and the smooth, "generalizing" distich form is the center of the poem. Similarly, "Alexis and Dora" gives an archetypal scene: a young man who discovers, just before departing on a long and dangerous voyage, that he loves a girl whom he has considered for years merely an acquaintance. She returns his love; he will devote the voyage to finding wealth for their life together. It is almost too idyllic, but the poem turns near its end to the jealousy which suddenly and fiercely overcomes the departing youth. The mood is broken, but the poet has avoided the danger of being merely typical by this one individual touch.

* There is of course a difficulty here: classical metrics depend mainly on quantity, German poetry primarily on stress. But since German does make a sharp distinction between "longs" and "shorts," it is less difficult to write good hexameters, say, in German than in English; though still far from easy.

TOWARD A NEW CLASSICISM

A third poem in distichs, "The Metamorphosis of Plants," has less emotional force but affords an exceptional insight into Goethe's unitary view of nature and man. With much detail, the poet instructs his beloved in the development of the plant from the seed through stalk, leaf, flower, and fruit. The "universal laws" are at work; the individual *is* the type. Similarly, their own relation has gone through the normal human metamorphoses from acquaintance through friendship to love. Man is part of nature, but, being uniquely self-conscious, he can help to determine his own growth.

More native in form, yet basically classical in spirit are two other important poems of these years, "General Confession" and "Permanence in Change." The former is one of a group of jovial drinking songs; the assembled group "confesses" that it has "Left undrunk / the brimming cup, / When it sparkled brightly . . ." As Goethe's poetry so often does, "General Confession" fuses seriousness and lightness. Rejecting asceticism and remorse, the singers vow:

> Uns vom Halben zu entwöhnen,
> Und im Ganzen, Guten, Schönen,
> Resolut zu leben.

> To give up half-measures and resolutely live
> in the whole, the good, the beautiful.

"Living resolutely" in this sense has well been called "the very center of Goethe's life as he strove to live it." The final stanza emphasizes, as the Victorian interpreters did not, that a resolute life includes the wholehearted enjoyment of wine and love. "Permanence in Change" explores the Heraclitan experience, poignantly familiar to Goethe: no one can swim twice in the same river. Yet the Muses have promised an imperishable gift: "The substance in your heart / And the form in your spirit"—the fusion in art of intellect and experience.

In a short poem explaining the intention of his idyllic epic (or epic idyll) *Hermann and Dorothea* (1797) Goethe disavowed any intention of vying with Homer; he was happy to be even the last of the Homerids. (The reference is to F. A. Wolf's theory, which shocked the poet, that the *Iliad* and the *Odyssey* were products of many hands.) Typically, he has found the positive aspect: now, without *hubris*, he can join the group of Homeric poets. Set against the background of the French Revolution, *Hermann and Dorothea* contrasts the solidity of patriarchal Germany to the chaotic world surrounding it. Fleeing from the Revolutionary armies, a miserable band of refugees is kindly welcomed by the citizens of a small German town, especially by Hermann and his family. The young man falls in love with one of the fugitives, the beautiful Dorothea. After some misunderstanding and reversals, they become engaged on the evening of the same day. While the surge of political events does afford a rough equivalent to the siege of Troy, Goethe had to get along without myths or gods. The only way to raise his narration to the classical plane was to make his main figures archetypal, and hence significant. This he has done: Hermann's family is made up of a loving, understanding mother, with the jealous father and the immature son opposing each other in a mildly Oedipal manner. The one person of heroic stature is Dorothea, who has performed feats of almost epic bravery during the trek of the *émigrés*. Revealingly, Goethe gave her a Greek name while the rather mediocre Hermann bears only a German one. From Homer he borrowed, besides his "optimistic way of seeing" (harvests are typically "abundant," the wine is "clear and splendid," and so forth) many stylistic devices, like the use of fixed epithets, extended metaphors, and the repetition of phrases and whole lines. (Of course he was well aware of the irony inherent in applying this style to middle-class citizens of a small town.) For the realistic aspects of the poem he drew upon the bourgeois idyll, especially on Voss's *Louise,* a once popular, quite philistine poem of contemporary domestic life. It is a strange combination, but the result is nevertheless successful.

Quite apart from the elements which made the poem immediately popular—its celebration of homely domestic virtue, an appealing story, sympathetic but humorous characterizations, and statement of a sturdy, conservative and non-aggressive patriotism—it has subtler qualities. The conciliatory, truly Goethean view of the Revolution is refreshing, and the irony of combining Homeric style with provincial life is delightful. No one is likely to find *Hermann and Dorothea* exciting, but its small-town, almost Biedermeier classicism has great charm.

Naturally, this attainment was not enough to satisfy Goethe's more serious classical ambitions. The fragment of his "Achilleis" (1799)—only one canto was completed—represents his attempt to compete with Homer in the full sense. The epic, in hexameters, was to be set between the actions narrated in the *Iliad* and the *Odyssey,* and to deal with Achilles' love for Polyxena, and his death. Clearly this is the most Faustian of Goethe's attempts to bring the past to life by writing as a Greek reborn. No mere curiosity of literary history, the fragment contains beautiful passages; but of course the difficulties of the undertaking were insuperable.

What may be called Goethe's hyperclassicism reached its climax in his commemorative essay "Winckelmann" (1805). Here the founder of the German cult of Greece appears as himself a pagan, a man who lived brilliantly and happily in the ancient style. Such men are seen as the goal of the universe:

> For of what use is the expenditure of suns and planets and moons, of stars and milky ways, of comets and nebulae, of developed and developing worlds, unless at last a happy man rejoices unconsciously in his own existence?

The essay was intended as a challenge to the rising romantic school, with its medievalizing, Germanizing, and Christianizing tendencies. What contemporary reader could have believed that its author was completing one of his most "German" works, the first part of *Faust* (see pages 132–176), at the very time he was writing this manifesto? Yet such was the complexity of Goethe's mind and sympathies. A high point of Goethe's classical endeavor, "Winckelmann" was written at a point when his genius was beginning to turn in another direction.

5. IRONY AND RENUNCIATION

SCHILLER'S DEATH, IN 1805, WAS A SEVERE SHOCK TO GOETHE, and it was only one of a host of troubles and crises. Two years before, Herder had died, estranged; there had been personal and intellectual tensions. Goethe, himself assailed by ill health, was rather isolated in the literary sphere, though for his artistic and antiquarian interests he still had a few staunch allies. While he pressed forward with studies of science, the lack of any favorable echo to his *Theory of Color* (1810) hurt him deeply.

The political world was equally unpleasant. After the defeat of the "invincible" Prussian army at Jena, in 1806, nearby Weimar was pillaged; Goethe's own home barely escaped. The Holy Roman Empire had come to an inglorious end the same year. No admirer of Prussia nor of the moribund Empire, the poet was nevertheless shaken. Even in Germany, the eighteenth century was coming to an end. Convinced that Napoleon was too great a genius to be defeated, and ambivalent about the surge of German nationalism during the so-called Wars of Liberation (1813–15), Goethe took no part in the patriotic literature of those days. After Napoleon had been defeated, he did write to be sure a patriotic "festival play," in effect apologizing for his aloofness; it contains the lines "Because of the suffering you felt / You are greater than I." They seem more graceful than deeply felt. Actually, he continued to admire Napoleon to the end of his life, convinced that the Emperor was a truly daemonic force, an authentic *Ur*-phenomenon.

About romanticism, the new wave of German literature, he was of two minds. Most of the German romantics admired or revered him; the Schlegels did much to spread his fame, not least through the elder Schlegel's influence on Mme. de Staël. Inevitably, Goethe was pleased when *Meister* was hailed as the apex of the novel, and he himself designated as "the representative of the spirit of poetry on this earth"; and he praised the few romantic efforts he thought sound, like the famous collection of folk songs, *The Boy's Magic Horn*. Most romantic tendencies, though, seemed anything but sound: glorification of the Middle Ages, expressions of (often unconvincing) Christian piety, nationalism, subjective idealism in philosophy, denigrations of classical art in the name of the Pre-Raphaelites. (The last infuriated him particularly.) Moreover, he had the largely correct impression that the new writers were too subjective and egotistic, full of "universal" projects that were never completed, irresponsible as men and as artists. In various essays and satiric poems he attacked them severely. But when *Faust I*, with its Northern-Gothic setting, appeared

IRONY AND RENUNCIATION

in 1808, and his novel, *The Elective Affinities*, the following year, many readers must have felt that the "great pagan" was becoming a romantic *malgré lui*. For while the novel attacked certain romantic tendencies, it displayed an interest in fanciful "natural philosophy" and religious art; and it could be read as a vindication of Christian ethics and belief.

Possibly *The Elective Affinities* is Goethe's finest novel: it has the symmetrical form of *Werther* but is the product of a maturer mind; it has the depth, if not the breadth of *Wilhelm Meister's Apprenticeship* and is a far more unified work of art. At the same time, *The Elective Affinities* is perhaps the most enigmatic work produced by Goethe's subtle, "dialectic" intelligence. Many readers have found the novel immoral; others, harshly rigoristic. Even the title seems ambiguous: affinities, as defined in the novel, are not truly "elective" but operate with the force of natural law. It may be that this baffling quality in the book kept it from having the impact of *Werther* or the influence of *Meister*. It has long fascinated novelists, critics, and scholars, though relatively neglected by general readers. Yet there are signs that *The Elective Affinities* is at last coming into its own. In an age with a taste for irony and difficulty in literature, this would not seem unnatural.

Briefly to indicate its content: two Germans of the upper class, Edward and Charlotte, live in leisure on their estate, in a contented if by no means ecstatic marriage. The arrival of a much younger woman, Ottilia, and of the Major* sets off the process of elective affinity:

* A few personages are designated only by title. The Major first appears as "the Captain" but is promoted in the due course of events.

Edward falls in love with Ottilia; the Major, with Charlotte; both loves are requited. Edward does not struggle against his passion, and Ottilia, though virtuous and well-behaved, cannot conceal hers. More restrained, the Major and Charlotte "renounce"—and soon are relegated to the background. When Edward later sleeps with his wife, each of them has the image of the beloved person in mind; the child of their "double adultery" combines features of Ottilia and the Major. After an unexpected and passionate encounter with Edward, Ottilia, distraught, lets Charlotte's baby fall into a lake on Edward's estate; it drowns despite her desperate efforts. After its death, Charlotte is willing to divorce Edward; but Ottilia believes that God has punished her, refuses to speak to Edward or the others, and manages to starve herself to death. She performs an apparent miracle in death, and a credulous multitude surrounds her coffin when she is laid out in the chapel. Edward dies soon after, and they are buried together.

This action is "distanced" by a style which is cool, formal, generally unemotional. While the "omniscient narrator" has strong sympathies for Ottilia, he shows a certain reserve at times, as in his repeated use of the word "seemed" in describing the alleged miracle. Generally he conveys praise or blame indirectly, merely recounting the actions and leaving the reader to draw his own conclusions.

As elsewhere, Goethe has transmuted unpromising raw material into art. In so doing, he manages also to preserve our sympathy for Edward and to make Ottilia's often neurotic behavior credible and at times admirable.

IRONY AND RENUNCIATION

The main riddles of the novel are moral ones: if marriage is absolutely sacred, why are one's sympathies intended to be with the lovers? Conversely, if they are justified, why must they perish? Also, why is the apostle of marriage Mittler ("Mr. Mediator") made so ridiculous? Critics have written of a collision between the natural law (the irresistible affinity) and the moral law (marriage). This is helpful to a point; but how can two laws collide in Goethe's unitary, harmonious universe? There are lesser puzzles: Ottilia is shown as noble and intelligent yet behaves strangely; Charlotte seems sensible and mature but tends to act unfortunately; Goethe, in comments on the book, both condemned and praised Edward. A final question, of the many which might be put, concerns the ending, which speaks of the lovers awaking together in another existence. Is this a conciliatory gesture toward sentimental readers, or more than that?

Some of these contradictions are only apparent: one should not assume that the point of view of the novel always conforms to Goethe's own; and that characters can be both admirable and deluded, worthy of both praise and blame, is hardly amazing. But the central problem, the relation of "elective affinity" to "moral law" cannot be evaded; I shall return to it.

Ottilia is the center of the novel. The narrator stresses her beauty and goodness repeatedly. Two of the minor characters are more or less in love with her. To bring out her sensitivity and intelligence, the narrator inserts several sections from her diary; these include some of Goethe's most penetrating aphorisms. (Aware that it would be straining our credulity too far to attribute all these insights to Ottilia, the author notes that some of them are not original with her.) Yet he does not shrink from showing her strange side—her mysterious headaches and ability to sense subterranean metals, for instance—which relates her to Mignon, though she is less pathological. In the uncanny closeness of her bond to Edward, the working of the elective affinity is made manifest. Involuntarily, she assumes his style of handwriting, even of playing the piano. She is tremendously sensitive, shy, and vulnerable; thus when she becomes conscious of her guilt, her self-punishment is total. Determined to chastise herself, she cuts herself off from all human intercourse. In committing suicide through starvation, she believes that she is obeying the command of the moral law. Thus she dies as a martyr of love.

The last fall days which the four spend together are marked by a sense of complete reconciliation. "No one felt resentful of another any longer; every sort of bitterness had disappeared." The aster, repeatedly used as a leitmotif, symbolizes the autumnal mood of the novel's closing.

In *The Elective Affinities,* Walther Killy has pointed out, no detail is insignificant. One might add that the placing of each detail is equally important. Anticipation, repetition, leitmotifs, and symbols are used more subtly because more sparsely than in the works of Mann—who was incidentally one of the greatest admirers of the book. Thus the motif of death by water is adumbrated more than once before the drowning of the infant. If the descriptions of parks, gardens, and trees seem inorganic, they are not really that: formal gardens, for example, reflect the orderliness of Charlotte; trees symbolize that sense of responsible tradition which Edward violates. When he impulsively makes heavy pencil marks across a map which the Major had drawn precisely and delicately, we learn a great deal about both men. Besides the symmetrical arrangement of the four main persons, there is a further balance between them and various contrast figures; thus Charlotte's worldly daughter Luciana is opposed to Ottilia; Edward's friends, the Count and the Baroness, live in cheerful adultery on the rim of the tragedy.

Dynamic and rather static sections are carefully balanced. Often a description of some part of Edward's estate will form a slow movement. The passages cited from Ottilia's diary have this function, as well as that of adding another dimension to her personality. At one point an inserted novella provides a double contrast: when the young hero saves the girl who really loves him from drowning, thus winning her away from her older fiancé, we have a sort of mirror image of Ottilia's situation as well as the reversal of the death-by-water motif.

Among Goethe's major works, *The Elective Affinities* is unique in that it was written with the conscious intention of stating an "idea" or major theme. The poet noted that this circumstance did not make it a better book; on the contrary, "the more incommensurable a poetic work, the more incomprehensible to the intellect (*Verstand*), the better." Yet to many of its readers, the novel does seem "incommensurable"—which naturally adds to its fascination.

To come back to the conflict between the moral and the natural law: in this life, the force of an authentic affinity is irresistible but the sanctity of marriage is absolute; therefore the lovers must perish. The rigorism of the book is sincere. At the same time, the narrator's sympathies, like the reader's, are increasingly with Ottilia and Edward. Contrast Goethe's treatment of them with Dante's of Paolo and Francesca; despite his feeling for them, the Italian poet relegated his lovers to Hell. In Goethe's novel, while love is thwarted if it conflicts with the norms of society, it still wins, paradoxically, a moral victory. To put it differently, there must be some plane on which moral and natural laws do not conflict. That is, I think, implied in the words about the lovers awaking together; they are not merely, or primarily, a concession to the reader. As at the end of *Faust II,* Goethe used familiar imagery here to suggest a very unconventional belief.

While striking a more "modern" note in *The Elective Affinities,* Goethe was not estranged, by any means, from his classical interests. The "festival play" *Pandora** (1808), combines contemporary reference with ancient myth, Greek and German elements, symbol and allegory, in a manner which anticipates the "Helen Act" of *Faust II.*

As Goethe's works so often do, *Pandora* contrasts two polar types of character. The Prometheus who appears here is not the artist-creator whom Goethe envisioned in the days of Storm and Stress; he is practical, realistic, concentrated on action. In fact, the smiths and warriors he commands seem to suggest the industrial masses of

---

* Actually, *Pandora* is only the first act of a projected drama, "Pandora's Return," which was never finished, but it is sufficiently complete in itself to be discussed as a separate entity.

IRONY AND RENUNCIATION

the rising nineteenth century. By no means ignoble, Prometheus has rejected, years before, the goddess Pandora; he has no relation to the idea of beauty she represents. Thereupon she turned to his brother Epimetheus, by whom she had two daughters. After her departure, Epimetheus is left in a state of poignant if fruitless longing. (His name, the "after-thinker," suggests one who reflects and meditates on the past; Prometheus, the "fore-thinker," is he who makes plans to shape the future.) In the contrast between them the alienation of spirit from power, particularly marked and dangerous in Germany, is reflected. The two Titans stand to each other as Schiller's realist to his idealist, or as the nineteenth-century Germans to the non-political generation before the Napoleonic wars—men who "thought a poem more important than a battle." If Prometheus recalls one side of Faust, Epimetheus is not too remote from Werther, or from Wilhelm Meister in his youth. Two different German traditions, often summed up in the names "Potsdam" and "Weimar," are represented in the brothers; neither is living in the sphere of "the whole, the good, and the beautiful"; there is no real communication between them; and if a synthesis is to be found, if Pandora is to return, the new generation must intervene.

This takes place in the love of Prometheus' son Phileros and Epimetheus' daughter Epimeleia ("the solicitous"). Each of them must undergo a symbolic ordeal of death and rebirth: Phileros by water, Epimeleia, like the Bajadere, by fire. (Kurt May has pointed out the analogy to *The Magic Flute*.) At the end of the act, Eos, the herald of the Olympians, speaks the crowning words:

while the Titans can make mighty beginnings, only the gods are the guides to "the eternally good, eternally fair"; let them prevail. This partial condemnation of the Titans implies also that their descendants will achieve the union of art and science, the ideal and the practical. Thus, even though Goethe never showed Pandora's return, he ends the act on a note of firm confidence; it is no mere fragment.

Pandora contains a wealth of forms and meters, ranging from classical trimeter to rhymed songs. Like *Faust,* it also makes use of music and symbolic setting. It is anything but dramatic: action is largely replaced by exposition, and its free use of allegory is not to everyone's taste. At times the style is so abstract that the language is forced and even stiff, but it also rises to some of the most moving lines Goethe ever wrote, as in this stanza of Epimetheus' lament:

> Wer von der Schönen zu scheiden verdammt ist,
> Fliehe mit abegewendetem Blick!
> Wie er, sie schauend, im tiefsten entflammt ist,
> Zieht sie, ach! reisst sie ihn ewig zurück.

> He who is condemned to part from the fair one / let him flee with averted face! / When he sees her, the depths of his being are inflamed— / she draws him, ah! she forces him back to her, eternally.

Poetry and Truth (1811–33), Goethe's autobiography, is itself a work of art. Combining poetic and literal actuality, the poet developed facts and incidents which still seemed important to him a generation later; only the sig-

IRONY AND RENUNCIATION

nificant detail, he believed, is really valid. Goethe organized his account of his life from birth to his departure to Weimar into four parts, each of which consists of five books. At least three of these parts have a clearly integrated form, though the claim that they are constructed like five-act dramas seems fanciful. Goethe used his material selectively, "heightening" events when that seemed appropriate; one cannot be sure for instance that his six-year-old reactions to the Lisbon earthquake were really those described in the book, but the philosophical impact of the disaster was so great that it had to be included. He consciously shifted his focus from himself to the world around him and back again. As in his dramas, he makes great use of "contrast figures"; they serve to bring out his own personality more sharply. In some cases, literary influences are evident: thus his account of his idyll with Friederike Brion is indebted to Goldsmith's *The Vicar of Wakefield*. Of course, there are various instances of a slip of memory. While his belief, clearly implied here, that each individual must find his proper style of life, relates *Poetry and Truth* to the educational novel, the book is not fiction but consciously stylized autobiography.

The first book begins, appropriately enough, with an account of the poet's birth which combines playful use of astrology with an implied sense of his own importance. "On the 28th of August, 1749, at the stroke of noon, I was born in Frankfurt on the Main. The constellation of the planets was favorable. . . ." A quality of self-acceptance marks the work; the tone is neither vain nor humble. As the poet put it later: "If Allah had wanted me to be a worm / He would have created me as one." Similarly, a note of restrained optimism marks his view of society and life as a whole. It is obvious, though it is not stressed, that most of the people he encountered liked Goethe; many of them loved him. In part, this brightness of tone is offset by ironic or pessimistic insights. Thus the Third Part bears the motto: "Provision has been made that the trees don't grow into the sky"; the Fourth: "Nemo contra deum nisi deus ipse."

Compared to, say, Rousseau's attitude in the *Confessions,* Goethe's view of himself and the world shows a certain ironical distance; this should not be mistaken for coldness. Convinced that lengthy introspection was dangerous, he keeps self-analysis to a minimum, reporting his emotions at a given point in his life objectively and concisely. Thus he can record even such matters as his sister's almost pathological devotion to him without breaking the serene flow of his style. There is a great deal of humor in *Poetry and Truth,* especially in the sections describing the poet's childhood. Of the various portraits of eccentric friends and acquaintances, perhaps the most memorable is that of a certain one-eyed skeptic Hüsgen, who liked to remark in a nasal voice: "Even in God I find mistakes." More central is Goethe's account of his ethical and philosophical development, his metamorphoses as it were. In Strasbourg he cured himself of fear of heights by climbing the spire of the great cathedral; other phobias were similarly overcome by conscious self-discipline. We read of his early doubts, of the impact of Herder and of Spinoza. Several pages are devoted to a sympathetic and charming retelling of some of the early books of the Old

IRONY AND RENUNCIATION

Testament. Partly this reflects the great formative influence of the Bible on his thought and language, but it is also clear that the tide of Goethe's "paganism" was ebbing. At the end of the book, the sense of fate which underlies and at times undercuts its genial optimism appears in the evocation of the daemonic forces by which man is ultimately controlled (see pages 11 f.).

It has often been said that Goethe was uninterested in history, and in fact he was more concerned with nature than with the study of the past as such, but this is only a partial truth; no one with his sense of gradual development could be really anti-historical. The opening books of *Poetry and Truth* show a keen interest in Frankfurt's medieval past and in the pageantry of the old empire. In the seventh book, autobiography recedes into the background; we have instead an account of German literary development in the eighteenth century which has been called the first literary history ever written and has been influential ever since, even in its prejudices. Similarly, his account of the impact of great French and British writers—Voltaire, Rousseau, Shakespeare—on his whole generation is invaluable.

Often Goethe will interrupt his narrative to make some moral generalization or other *aperçu*. Its leisurely pace allows him to make various excursuses, including even a fairy tale of his own invention. His intention was to provide a panorama as well as a self-portrait. Not only has he shown his own efforts "to raise the pyramid of my existence ever higher" (as he wrote in another context) but he has given us a broad sense of the scope and the metamorphoses of German culture during a crucial period.

In a sense the *Italian Journey* (1816 ff.) is a continuation of *Poetry and Truth;* it too is autobiography and something more. Here too there is a double focus; his own ideas and sensations are combined with an inclusive account not only of works of art and Mediterranean landscapes but of popular mores and festivals, religious practices, even of Italian methods of agriculture. Perhaps inevitably, the book does not have the charm and warmth of his account of his own culture, and as the record of his search for a specific goal it is more limited and self-conscious than *Poetry and Truth.*

The stream of Goethe's lyrical production was never exhausted. Like the river in "Mohammed's Song" it might be diminished but never checked in its flow. Naturally, Goethe being Goethe, it ran highest when the poet was in love, or was trying to purge himself of a hopeless or dangerous passion. Fortunately for us, such moments were frequent.

While the "Sonnets" of 1808 contain one or two powerful poems, they are largely half-serious exercises in mastering yet another sort of poetry. Here, as Staiger suggests, lies their main interest: the poet, having in a sense exhausted the possibilities of one form after another, looks for new difficulties to overcome. Many of the verses written in the decade after the "Sonnets" are epigrammatic or gnomic; a few, more lyric, should be mentioned here. At times, a note of intensity is heard in verses which are otherwise rather light. Thus the poet, feeling himself surrounded by the dilettantes and insensitive readers of the new generation, bursts out: "Where's just one, who bears the torment / Of the load which we have carried?". "At Midnight" is less translucent than most of Goethe's poems; it has a haunting, enigmatic quality; it "is" more than it "means." Three stanzas evoke midnight scenes; the frightened boy is afraid of the cemetery he must pass but rejoices in the beauty of the stars; the youth visits his love; the mature man reflects, in the light of the full moon, on the past and the future. Goethe noted that he did not know the poem's intention himself and was all the fonder of it for that reason.

Belatedly, the *West-Easterly Divan* (*Westöstlicher Divan,* 1819; the title is hard to translate acceptably) has been recognized as one of Goethe's greatest works. Contrary to his general practice, the poet organized these lyrics into a cycle of twelve "books"—not all of them are complete—and published them as an independent volume. The poems include love lyrics, epigrammatic reflections, invectives, songs in praise of wine, and philosophical poetry. The basic fiction is that the lyrical "I" appears behind the mask of the poet Hatem, who expresses his emotions and thoughts, above all his love for Zuleika, who responds in verses of her own.

Following Herder and Friedrich Schlegel, various romantic poets and scholars were turning to Indian and Persian themes. Goethe had himself been interested in Oriental thought and poetry since the days when he had written "Mohammed's Song." Stimulated by recent translations of Hafiz and Firdusi, he returned to Eastern material, following the romantic lead; but he treated it more clearly, lightly, and ironically than did his contemporaries. While he felt that Indian and Egyptian mythology was grotesque, he found the Persian myths graceful and orderly, and thus at least relatively classic.

Goethe's symbolic flight to the East has been compared to his actual flight to Italy. In this case, he was escaping from public, not private troubles: he began to write the *Divan* poems in 1814, late in the struggle against Napoleon, which filled him with dismay rather than with enthusiasm, and with the wish to withdraw to a calmer sphere. The first poem, "Hegira," strikes the note of escape: the kingdoms of this world are falling apart, thrones are collapsing; the poet will seek rejuvenation in the "patriarchal air" of the undisturbed, and hence "pure" Orient.

The title of the *Divan* testifies to a broad cosmopolitanism which is a welcome contrast both to the chauvinism of the times and to Goethe's own rather exclusive classicism of the 1790's. It is in line with his emerging concept of world literature:

> To God belongs the Orient!
> To God belongs the Occident!
> Northern, like the southern lands,
> Rest peacefully within his hands.

Beyond this, the title affords a useful key to the understanding of these sophisticated, rather difficult poems. The lyric "Gingko Biloba" symbolizes the nature of the entire cycle: unity in duality, East and West combined yet each preserving its essence; the poet, like the gingko leaf, is both "single and double." Similarly, the poems are

IRONY AND RENUNCIATION

both serious and ironic; both intellectual and emotional; the speaker is both Hatem and the "real" Goethe; the love celebrated here contains happiness and resignation. More: there is even a dual authorship, for some of the most striking lyrics of the *Divan,* attributed to "Zuleika," were actually written by Marianne von Willemer, whom Goethe loved first playfully, then very seriously, in the years when the *Divan* was being composed.

Marianne, formerly an actress and dancer, was the protégée of Goethe's old friend Willemer, who married her shortly after the poet had first met her. She was charming, pretty, Austrian; she even wrote verses, though no one could have foreseen that she would become a genuine poet during the time of her love for Goethe—and only during that time. Their passion was strong, but remained "Platonic"; Willemer seems to have behaved with admirable *savoir vivre,* and Goethe, frightened by the strength of his own emotions, avoided seeing Marianne after knowing her for some two years, though a correspondence was continued. The paradox of a love which is requited but not fulfillable accounts for much of the dual, "single and double" tone of the *Divan.*

To a public which still expected a confessional, "sincere" note in lyric poetry, the *Divan* was baffling; in fact, the book was not really appreciated until the twentieth century. Irony, distance, boldness of diction, even plays on words—what was the "general reader" to make of them? While the confessional note is still heard (as it always is in Goethe's poetry) it is now muted. Following the precept of his maturity, "Shape, artist, do not speak," Goethe had moved very far beyond contemporary taste.

"Empty formalism" and "lyricism of old age" are clichés which were often applied to the *Divan* during the nineteenth century. Apparently most readers were insensitive to the intellectual zest of this symbolic adventure, in which the poet rode into distant lands "with only the stars over my cap," feeling that he had come into a great inheritance: "Time is my possession, the field I plow is time." Without being pious, Hafiz is blessed—to the great annoyance of scribes and Philistines. With this exuberance goes a sense of renewed youth within maturity; half-seriously, Goethe calls himself (or Hatem) a "lively ancient":

> What if your hair is white,
> You still shall love.

As the land of the patriarchs, the Orient is the land of eternity, of the ever-repeated pattern:

> Dein Lied ist drehend wie das Sterngewölbe,
> Anfang und Ende immerfort dasselbe,
> Und was die Mitte bringt ist offenbar
> Das was zu Ende bleibt und anfangs war.
>
> Your song revolves like the starry vault, / beginning and end evermore the same, / and what the center brings is manifestly / what lasts till the end and was in the beginning.

It is no accident that the stars form a frequent motif in the *Divan,* symbols of permanence and yet of ordered change, or that tension between eternity and the moment is a recurring theme. Zuleika, standing before the mirror,

IRONY AND RENUNCIATION

knows that her beauty will fade, but at this instant it reflects a timeless beauty: "Before God everything must stand eternal / Love Him in me, for this moment." Similarly, in the poem "Song and Formed Image," Goethe uses his familiar river symbol to suggest the flux of time —and also, in this instance, the evanescence of poetry, compared to the static quality of Greek art. Yet by the act of aesthetic creation, the flow can be halted: "When the poet's pure hand draws it up / Water forms a sphere."

As always, there is a place for change and rebirth within the pattern of permanence. The most magnificent poem of the *Divan*, "Holy Longing," presents the longing for rebirth in the metaphor of sexual love:

>Sagt es niemand, nur den Weisen,
>Weil die Menge gleich verhöhnet,
>Das Lebendge will ich preisen
>Das nach Flammentod sich sehnet.
>
>In der Liebesnächte Kühlung,
>Die dich zeugte, wo du zeugtest,
>Überfällt dich fremde Fühlung
>Wenn die stille Kerze leuchtet. . . .
>
>Und so lang du das nicht hast,
>Dieses: Stirb und werde!
>Bist du nur ein trüber Gast
>Auf der dunklen Erde.

Tell it to no one, only to the wise, / for the mob at once sneers, / I will praise the living being / who longs for a fiery death.

> In the cooling of nights of love— / which begat you, where you begat— / a sense of strangeness overcomes you / when the silent candle shines. . . .
> And as long as you do not possess it / this: Die and be reborn! / You are only a troubled guest / on the dark earth.

Goethe's fusion of love and death reminds one of the romantic notion of the *Liebestod* but is really very different. In Wagner or Novalis, the "love-death" expresses a longing for Schopenhauerian nothingness or for ecstasy gained by the Dionysiac loss of individuality. For this, the sexual act as such is the appropriate symbol. For Goethe, the ecstasy has the aim of metamorphosis to a higher form: the embrace leads to the conception of a new being; dying, to new life.

Although none of Marianne's poems approaches the splendor of "Holy Longing," a few of her love lyrics are memorable, and Goethe did not hesitate to include them in the *Divan*. She performed an amazing feat of empathy, while maintaining an authentic feminine note; for a time, Marianne actually was metamorphosed into a poet.

The *Divan* represents the most striking, though by no means the last, of Goethe's lyrical rejuvenations. When "Hatem" writes that his heart is unchanging, youthful, raging like Etna under its snow and clouds, his irony is basically serious. Recently there has been a tendency to rank the *Divan* next to *Faust* in the Goethean canon. The case for this is a good one.

While the *Divan*, in Goethe's usual fashion, keeps its potentially tragic element muted, the poem "Pariah" has as its theme one of those harsh and violent conflicts which he usually avoided: it deals with a radical break in man's

IRONY AND RENUNCIATION

nature, with a "volcanic" element in life. The legend must have oppressed Goethe; he kept it in mind for some forty years before giving it final form. In the first of three parts, the miserable pariah prays to Brahma for a mediator. The second tells of the fall, after a symbolic seduction, of the seemingly irreproachable wife of a Brahman; her husband beheads her. Hastily her loyal son tries to reunite her head with her body by magic, but inadvertently joins it to the torso of a woman criminal. (Compare Mann's legend, *The Transposed Heads*.) It is a radical symbol of her, and man's, dual nature; she is no more invulnerable than the pariah to the pull of the senses, for no one can resist a seduction ordained by the gods. The last brief section contains the pariah's thanks to Brahma: all are equal in his sight. Most untypical of Goethe, "Pariah" seems to state the existence of an element of radical evil in all men; in that sense, it is a Christian poem.

In its triadic structure, but in no other way, Goethe's "Trilogy of Passion" (1823–24) recalls "Pariah"; it is directly, almost overwhelmingly, confessional. More than seventy years old, he had fallen in love with a nineteen-year-old girl.* Etna was raging again. He proposed marriage, with the Duke himself as his intermediary. While the girl refused this somewhat bizarre offer, it is probably revealing that she never married. For the last time, and with express reference to Werther and Tasso, Goethe poured his disappointed passion into poetry.

The first part indeed is called "To Werther." Written in rhymed stanzas of varying length, it shows a careful correctness of versification and smoothness of rhythm

* Ulrike von Levetzow.

unusual in Goethe's very late poetry; it is as if the poet were trying to balance the explosive power of his passion by putting particular stress on form. In its fusion of emotion with moral reflection, "Trilogy of Passion" recalls "Dedication" and some of the other poems to Charlotte, but the emotion is stronger, the tone much darker. "To Werther" gives a somber profile of life: it "seems a splendid lot" but is actually a series of crises and errors. "Warned first too early, then too late," man comes to realize that life is a leave-taking, a departure, whether from love or from existence itself. Werther lost little by his early death; man's only hope is that a god may grant him the power to express his sufferings.

This reminiscence of *Tasso* forms a bridge to the second section, "Elegy," where it is repeated in varied form. The tone grows darker, the situation more specific. Wishing not to forget, but to be able to endure his loss, the poet tries to conjure up the image of all that remains:

> Ist denn die Welt nicht übrig? Felsenwände,
> Sind sie nicht mehr gekrönt von heiligen Schatten?
> Die Ernte, reift sie nicht? Ein grün Gelände,
> Zieht sichs nicht hin am Fluss durch Busch und
>   Matten?

> Does the world no longer exist? Walls of rock, / are they no longer crowned by holy shadows? / The harvest, does it not ripen? The green tract of land, / does it not stretch along by the river, through bushes and meadows?

He recalls the courageous serenity of his love's way of living, but none of these efforts brings any consolation. There is even a hint of suicide. At the end, the poet, who

IRONY AND RENUNCIATION

was but recently "the darling of the gods" feels like Tasso that he has lost everything, even himself. The gods have bestowed a Pandora upon him; the gift was a fatal one, and the "Elegy" culminates in the words "and they destroy me."

In three stanzas the final section, "Reconciliation," states the resolution. "The lost heart stiffens and rejoices," as T.S. Eliot put it. In Goethe's poem, it is the soaring of music, weaving its millions of notes together, which makes the heart sense that it is still alive, and wish to continue living in gratitude. The "Trilogy" is the last towering pinnacle of that vast edifice of lyric poetry which Goethe built, year after year, during more than half a century.

Goethe's last novel, *Wilhelm Meister's Wanderjahre** (1829), is most interesting, I believe, as a repository of his ideas about society and education, of his wisdom. Often it is compared to that other vast product of his later years, *Faust II*. While it is true that the active, individualistic ethos of *Faust* and the more collectivist, altruistic ideal of the *Wanderjahre* are complementary, the comparison is basically misleading. *Faust*, after all, is above all a poem—Faust's opinions are "not necessarily the author's"—but this novel is primarily a didactic one. As various ironies indicate, Goethe has little interest here in "telling a story" (except in the inserted novellas) or in presenting rounded, "real" characters. Also, he apparently lost interest in Meister himself as the composition of the *Wanderjahre* proceeded. It may be regretted that he de-

---

* The translation "Travels" distorts the meaning of the title.

cided to yoke his views on social matters to the *Meister* theme. In his old age, Goethe often treated the conventions of authorship with sovereign indifference. Some sections of the novel were actually written by his assistants Eckermann and Riemer; another was taken over unchanged from his faithful follower Heinrich Meyer. Largely dictated, the book often reveals in its style a certain stiffness and dryness. The poet himself called it "a collective product," "a peculiar opus," and stated frankly that "the plot about the hero is only a sort of string that runs through it"; the book appeared to him as an agglomeration rather than a unity, but its point of view, he said, was a single one. But about such major themes of the book as renunciation, the "reverences," and the holiness of labor (which so appealed to Carlyle) he was deeply serious. Here the major values of the *Wanderjahre* may be found.

Years before, at about the time he finished his novel of apprenticeship, Goethe had written to Schiller that its very title demanded its correlative, mastery; later, he even thought, perhaps not too seriously, of a third novel to round out the development. At any rate, the first version of the *Wanderjahre* did not appear until a quarter of a century after this remark. It would be amazing if the "unsuspected principles of form" which Hofmannsthal divined in the novel had really determined its shape. It is best not to take the book as an aesthetic structure, but as a document: a reaction against romantic individualism and dilettantism, and on the practical plane against European overpopulation and depression; a turn toward the acceptance of a collective organization of society. In the final version, America appears as the last best hope of mankind; the great aim is to transplant the values of culture to the New World while leaving Europe's disadvantages behind.

As far as conventional narrative is concerned, Goethe treats the plot almost with disdain. He teases the reader in various ways, intervening to tell him that certain facts cannot yet be revealed, to note that it is difficult to keep all the female characters straight, and so on. One cannot easily recognize in Wilhelm the hero of the *Apprenticeship*: his marriage seems a most unreal relationship, his new profession—surgery—comes as a complete surprise, and whether or not he attains his goal, or erstwhile goal, of culture now seems a matter of slight importance. Bound by a curious oath to stay no more than three days in one place, he wanders about until finally released from this obligation. In fact, his story is interrupted by no fewer than nine novellas, and the insertion of numerous letters adds to its fragmented quality. There is a curious distinction between different groups of characters: those already known from the *Apprenticeship* are seen historically, as real people long known to the reader; those in the novellas have the usual status of fictional personages, though the two types are brought together at the end.

It is largely the interplay between the story proper and the nine novellas which determines the structure. Of these, almost all have a thematic relation to the main action: motifs of wandering, of marriage and love, of renunciation, and of work are developed. At the end of the version of 1829, as if to demonstrate his indifference to the form of the novel as such, Goethe added a series of aphorisms and a poem linked most loosely to the novel. In *Meister's Apprenticeship,* Gundolf has pointed out, elements like Mignon's songs or the discussions of Shakespeare are integral parts of the novel; here this is not the case. The *Wanderjahre* should be compared, not to other novels, but to Utopian literature in the line of Plato's *Republic.*

To turn to the real burden of the book, its didactic content: on the plane of the individual's life it fully develops the theme of renunciation already stated in *Tasso, The Elective Affinities,* "Trilogy of Passion," and elsewhere. For many years, Goethe struggled, like Faust, against the knowledge that man must repeatedly give up what he has most cherished and desired. Now he accepts the necessity of resignation, and by showing it in many aspects—the subtitle of *Meister's Wanderjahre* is "The Renouncers"—tries to distill positive value from the harsh experience of deprivation.

Thus Wilhelm himself has renounced his intellectual ambitions and even his life with Natalia. Similarly, the lovers in the *Wanderjahre* are generally separated or otherwise frustrated. The tone is somber indeed, though in some cases there are hints of final reunion after the ordeal has been passed. If an individual can sacrifice himself for the sake of a larger good, he can achieve a measure of happiness. When a serene, well-adjusted person appears in Goethe's later works, it has been remarked, he is generally one who has renounced. As we shall see, the theme affects the ideas of education presented in the book, and even its economic notions.

Early in the *Wanderjahre,* Wilhelm is told that "now

IRONY AND RENUNCIATION

it's the era of one-sidedness"—in other words, the nineteenth century. Pliant as he normally is, he accepts the dictum unquestioningly, just as he had accepted the universal ideal of the previous age. Man, it now appears, reaches fulfillment only within strict limits, in a specialized craft or profession, and Wilhelm finds a vocation which is both altruistic and humane.

In fact, society in the *Wanderjahre* is organized collectively: men band themselves together, pooling their special talents, whether for emigration or some other undertaking. No systematic theory of society is attempted, but the general implication is clear: the individual alone can no longer cope with the world. In place of the charmingly relaxed and leisurely sphere of the earlier novel, we have a realm of work, diligence, collective effort. The time is out of joint; determined, disciplined labor may not put it right, but it will at least enable some men to lead a decent if austere existence.

This austerity is mitigated, however, in a very Goethean way: by music and especially by song. Craftsmen, emigrants, and the students in the "Pedagogical Province" are forever singing, generally in a mood of cheerful resoluteness. Although the bonds of the old order are broken and human confidence has been violated, the wanderers chant their refrain: "Let your striving be in love / Let your life be the deed." In showing the metamorphoses of contemporary society, Goethe seems to urge that as much as possible of the old patriarchal element be retained. The book does not propose a romantic return to the past but rather a gradual, not a "volcanic" development. If men must leave their old ways and homes, it is all the more important that inner, centripetal forces be kept strong.

Gradually it becomes apparent that not only Wilhelm but all of society is wandering. There are even itinerant governments and peripatetic police forces. Goethe has completely reversed the favorite romantic motif of *Wanderlust*; his characters "wander" or travel for some serious reason, moral or economic. A great goal of these groups is practical success; every moment must be used to the full; all work is strictly supervised, but their crafts are ennobled with the name of the "serene arts." Written like Keats' "Ode to a Nightingale" under the impact of economic depression, the last version of the book recommends emigration as a sensible escape from the malaise of the old world. Renouncing the past, one group of emigrants sets out for America, another attempts "inner colonization" in an under-developed European province.

On another plane, the "Pedagogical Province," a school for boys and young men, actually an autonomous little country, tries to cope practically with the new era. The school combines practical and humanistic goals; at one stage, the boys divide their time between horse-raising and the study of modern languages. (Needless to say, the school is a symbolic, more or less Utopian institution; not every detail should be taken literally.) Throughout there is an attempt to mediate between extremes; discipline is combined with the joy of learning; *esprit de corps* is cultivated, but the students do not wear uniforms. One building is devoted in part to "symphronistic" friezes picturing parallel events or myths of various cultures,

IRONY AND RENUNCIATION

expressing the same basic truth in various ways—a sort of general education. In the section of the Province devoted to the education of future artists, the training is particularly severe. Really gifted students understand the necessity of discipline, for "art is called art precisely because it is not nature"; it must be learned. Here the aesthetic education of future musicians, painters, sculptors, architects, and poets takes place. There is one omission: actors and dramatic poets are banned, for the mimic art involves insincerity. Alas for Wilhelm and his theatrical mission! —and the author himself admits that he finds this aspect of the curriculum strange and harsh.

While various features of the Province, especially the banishment of one type of artist for moral reasons, recall the *Republic,* the general scheme is not Platonic. As Viëtor shows, the school is not martial, not concerned with an elite, not really political. Its central concern is religious and ethical training; the intellect is a secondary concern. All discipline is based on the pupils' sense of honor. Above all a sense of reverence or awe (*Ehrfurcht*) is inculcated. The pupils learn reverence for what is above us, like us, and beneath us—the three stages corresponding to "ethnic" religion (like the Greek cult of the Olympians): the religion of the sages; and Christianity,* with its emphasis on pity. In synthesis, these produce a true reverence for oneself, parallel to the universal,

---

* Christ's life on earth is part of the "religion of the sages"; His sufferings and death, of the third stage. While the pupil is told, at the end of his studies, of the Crucifixion, the masters of the Province consider it "execrable" to display the Cross. Such mysteries, almost unbearably painful, should not be vulgarized.

all-embracing religion. Thus the student is gradually led to a self-acceptance free of conceit and selfishness.

The strange figure of Makaria ("The Blessed One") is the metaphysical center, as it were, of *Meister's Wanderjahre*. Just as the poet has within him the elements of poetry, this sibylline woman, we are told, has a sort of spiritual model of the solar system within herself. At the same time she is herself a part of the major system of stars and planets, and moves in a spiral (Goethe's favorite image of "heightening") relative to the sun. The imagery is bizarre but its purport becomes clear when one recalls Kant's famous statement that two things filled him with awe: the starry heavens above and the moral law within. Thus Makaria's entelechy or indestructible inner form mirrors and is in a sense identical with the law of the cosmos. Here, as in Schiller's *Wallenstein*, the stars are symbols of order and permanence. This interpretation of the *Wanderjahre* is borne out by the poem "Testament," which appears at a strategic point in the book. It declares in lapidary sentences that no real essence can be destroyed, for being is eternal and follows unchanging laws. As the earth and its brethren revolve about the sun, a similar order exists within men:

> Denn das selbständige Gewissen
> Ist Sonne deinem Sittentag.

For the independent conscience / is the sun of your moral day.

In Schiller's sense, Makaria is an authentic "beautiful soul," in whom duty and inclination coincide. Living

IRONY AND RENUNCIATION

primarily on a spiritual plane, she nevertheless plays her practical role in the world kindly and effectively. Further to emphasize the wisdom of this saintly Sibyl, Goethe has attributed to her a series of maxims and aphorisms which are included in the work.

With its stress on renunciation, altruism, and the conscience, the *Wanderjahre* is the most Christian of Goethe's major works. Its Christian quality however is non-dogmatic, tempered by the humanism of Weimar. Thus Makaria notes in her collection of adages: "It would not be worthwhile to live to be seventy years old if all the wisdom of this world were foolishness before God." At the end of the novel proper, Wilhelm, now accomplished in his profession, revives his son Felix after he has nearly drowned. This brings the long story of his education to a close: finally, within his chosen limits, he has achieved mastery. Looking at the body of his son, he exclaims on how man, "splendid in God's image," is created again and again, though always threatened by dangers. Thus the work ends with an affirmation of the eternal archetypes.

Written in the Christian mood of *Meister's Wanderjahre*, Goethe's "Novella" (1827) is a symbolic tale in which human passions are reflected in a near-miraculous action. (To Goethe, a novella was basically the narration of "an unheard-of event.") In the story a lion and tiger, and the conflagration which has allowed them to escape, provide the symbols of passion. Secretly in love with the wife of his prince, the young courtier Honorio "saves" her by killing the tiger, only to be told that the animal was harmless. Rather than trying to slay the lion, it is decided to let a child try to charm him with the music of a flute; the child succeeds, and removes a thorn from his paw; the novella ends on a note of peace and harmony. The motif of Daniel in the lion's den has been fused with that of Androcles. In Goethe's words, the tale intends "to show how the untamable, unconquerable element is often better mastered through piety and love than through violence." Less obvious is the symbolic aspect: the animals and the fire mirror one side of Honorio's nature; the blameless child, the other; and the final resolution is an image of his own self-conquest. The story is written in a deceptively simple way; generalized characters move and act in an archetypal, timeless landscape. Possibly a certain Biedermeier note in the depiction of human society detracts somewhat from the universality of its reference.

In the following year Goethe's lyrical genius welled up for the last time. The so-called "Dornburg poems" (1828) —"The Betrothed," "To the Rising Full Moon," and "Early, Vale and Hills and Garden" are marked by recollected emotion rather than the passion of the "Trilogy." Highly concentrated and symbolic, almost impossible to interpret adequately, all three express a final affirmation.

An earlier poem, "Primal Words. Orphic," states Goethe's mature view of the world with the utmost concentration. Each of the five "primal concepts"—Daemon, Chance, Love, Necessity, Hope—is developed in a stanza; the tone is lofty, even oracular. Proceeding dialectically, the poem shows how each original force is modified by others: thus the Daemon (the fundamental innate character of each individual) is affected but not thwarted by

IRONY AND RENUNCIATION

Chance (the influence of others and of the milieu); Hope offsets Necessity. Two lines—"And no time, no power can disintegrate / a firmly stamped form, developing as it lives"—express a conviction which is central to Goethe's thought, especially to *Faust*, his crowning achievement.

6. FAUST I: THE LITTLE WORLD

Faust IS SO VAST, ITS IMPORT HAS BEEN SO LONG DISCUSSED and debated, that anyone who tries to write about it today should make clear the bases and presuppositions of his own interpretation. First, despite the many autobiographical elements, Faust is not Goethe. When Faust sums up his life near the end of the drama—

> I have only galloped through the world
> And clutched each lust and longing by the hair;
> What did not please me, I let go,
> What flowed away, I let it flow.

—no sensible person will apply these magnificent lines to the poet's career. After all, Goethe is also reflected in a number of very un-Faustian personages: Tasso, Wilhelm Meister, Hatem, even Mephistopheles. This does not deny Faust's closeness to what one imagines to be the "real" Goethe at many points: when he addresses the "sublime

FAUST I: THE LITTLE WORLD

spirit" in the scene "Forest and Cavern" for instance, or when he sets out to win Helen. The two considerations do not cancel each other out.

Second, one cannot understand *Faust I* without reading the second part—or knowing, at the very least, what takes place there. Part I begins by setting Faust's whole career into a cosmic frame: God and Mephistopheles* debate the question: what shall become of a person like Faust, "a good man with his dark urges," in this world and the next? The ensuing scenes are largely concerned with Faust's philosophical question—which is at the same time a very personal one—how is he to live without finding an authentic insight into reality? But to the unfortunate reader who does not go beyond *Faust I*, the end of it all is anti-climactic. Very early in his great quest, Faust is responsible for the downfall of a naive girl and the destruction of her family; he tries to save her from prison but must flee with Mephisto; a "voice from above" declares that the girl is saved; Part I closes. The reader who goes no further often feels a sense of disappointment. Since Part II is not "difficult" poetry by twentieth-century standards, there is all the more reason to persevere.

Should one read the vast drama as a unity, or focus on its various sections and stages in terms of what we know about Goethe at the time he wrote each? Much is to be said for the latter course. The composition of the poem extended over at least sixty years, and Goethe's attitude toward it changed repeatedly. Not only is the tone of Part II very different from that of *Faust I*; there are

---

* Hereafter to be called, less formally, "Mephisto."

certain puzzling inconsistencies. Without difficulty one can show that this speech is characteristically Storm and Stress, that scene reflects Weimar classicism, another is romantic. At times Faust sounds like Herder or Rousseau, at others like Spinoza. And so on.

Against these arguments the "unitarians" submit various rebuttals. The most valid one for the general reader is pragmatic: the poem is *there*, it must stand on its own feet. Read it hypothetically, as a unity, and see what you get! If one has to know a great deal about Goethe's life and the various "isms" of literary history to understand *Faust*, that in itself indicates a sharp limitation of the work. There is a certain broad unity in the poem, based largely on Faust's character; it possesses an overarching harmony more important than its dissonances. To be sure, one must draw on specialized knowledge to understand a few passages; above all, the more one knows about Goethe, his times, and the Faust legend, the better. The drama was not written in a vacuum nor for the uneducated, but it was intended for cultivated readers, not for specialists.

Why did Goethe call *Faust* a tragedy? Since the Second World War, several interpreters have taken "tragedy" in its most pessimistic sense, emphasizing Faust's ruthlessness and his many offenses, and casting doubt on his right to salvation. In part, this was a reaction against nineteenth-century optimism and Fascist activism, particularly the perverted "Faustianism" of the Nazis. One acute critic has boldly read the last scene—Faust's ascension—as a dream or illusion of the dying hero. Neither the poem itself, however, nor Goethe in his comments

FAUST I: THE LITTLE WORLD

about it, expresses any doubt that Faust is saved; and, given the very optimistic presuppositions of the "Prologue," he deserves to be. (Whether he would be content in a Christian heaven is, as Santayana noted, another matter.) After all, a tragedy need not end "unhappily": one has only to think of *Oedipus at Colonus* and the *Eumenides*.

One might say that *Faust* is a long dramatic poem with some epic and many lyric features. With its use of music, spectacle, symbolic setting, a tremendous range of poetic meters—there is even a scene in prose—*Faust* embodies that "progressive universal poetry" which the critic Friedrich Schlegel called for. It is equally "universal," in his sense, that *Faust* is now serious, now comic, now satiric, that it is both classical and contemporary, and that the second part comments upon and elucidates the first, often in an ironic way.

In yet a third way *Faust* approaches universality: in the course of writing it, Goethe drew abundantly on his vast reading. Thus the "Prelude" in Part I was suggested by Kalidasa's drama *Sakuntala*, the "Prologue in Heaven" by Job, Gretchen in her madness recalls Ophelia. The notion, basic to the whole shape of the play, of Faust's soul as an indestructible, upward-striving monad, is Leibnizian. For *Faust II*, Goethe employed the European tradition of 3,000 years with sovereign freedom, ranging from Homer to Byron. Throughout, it is a matter of the creative reshaping of inherited material.

This is not the place to explore the richness of the Faust legend and the material related to it or to recount what has been recorded of the historical Dr. Johann Faust.* Thematically it is linked to the myth of the magus, to tales of a variety of sorcerers, from antiquity onward. The so-called Spies *Faustbook* (1587) is in effect the warning of the Reformation against Renaissance lust for knowledge. Marlowe's great drama is ambivalent in its attitude toward the magician: he holds the author's sympathies, but is irrevocably damned for all that. By the eighteenth century, the Faust theme had sunk to the level of chapbooks and puppet plays. To the ordinary "Enlightened" mind the subject was barbarous, but one of the most extraordinary men of the Enlightenment, Lessing, took it up nevertheless. Moreover, he reversed the course of the action: the Faust of his drama (of which only fragments exist) was to be saved, for "the Almighty did not give man the noblest of his drives [the thirst for knowledge] in order to make him eternally unhappy. . . ." (One notes that Goethe's Faust is in search of all experience, not of knowledge alone.)

At least since the early nineteenth century, the psychological link between Faust's universal dynamism and the specifically erotic activism of Don Giovanni has been seen. A lesser figure, Peter Schlemihl, deserves brief mention: this semi-Faustian hero sells not his soul but his shadow (his reputation?). While the nineteenth century produced a superabundance of "thralls to Faust," it could not exhaust the subject, as Thomas Mann's novel and Valéry's incomplete drama remind us.

* See the bibliography, especially the books by Palmer and More and E. M. Butler.

FAUST I: THE LITTLE WORLD

Three introductory sections—"Dedication," "Prelude in the Theater," and "Prologue in Heaven"—form a triple-arched gateway to the drama. "Dedication," a poem in *ottava rima*, is rather melancholy in tone: the poet, recalling the beginnings of *Faust* a quarter of a century before,[*] addresses "elusive shapes," its characters. Associated with them are memories of friends now dead or scattered about the world. With a sense of resolution, the short poem ends with the statement that while immediate actuality recedes into the distance, the once-lost visions are becoming realities again.

Accordingly, the scene "Prelude in the Theater" is indeed more realistic. Two of its three characters, the Director and the Clown, are very much down to earth. If the third, the Theater Poet, is a romantic, recalling perhaps Wilhelm Meister in youth, the Director, a practical man of affairs, may remind us of Antonio, while the Clown's rather cynical wit anticipates Mephisto's. The verse form is freer—rhymed iambics with four or five accents to a line. In tone it varies from the lyric soaring of the Poet to the robustness of the Clown; but it is characteristic of *Faust* that each speaker has at least a few lines of exalted poetry. A play is about to begin; the Director consults his associates, very much at the last moment, about the coming production. The Poet eloquently states the glories and miseries of his calling; the Clown demands color, variety, and above all comedy; the Director presses vigorously for action. From the point

[*] For an account of Goethe's earlier treatments of the theme (the "Urfaust," and the "Fragment" of 1790) see such standard works as Bielschowsky's and Viëtor's.

of view of *Faust* as a whole, each of the three is right up to a point and has his aspect of the truth. This "dialectical" situation is again typical: very rarely is a character completely right or utterly wrong. At the end, the Director bids his assistants to "move with deliberate speed / From Heaven through the world to Hell."

Thus a bridge has been built to the "Prologue in Heaven," poetically the first high point of Faust. The stage reveals God with the heavenly hosts; the three archangels step forward. Their magnificent song makes it clear that the poem is set against the background of the whole cosmos. Singing first, Raphael sets the tone of splendor and praise:

> The sun-orb sings, in emulation,
> 'Mid brother-spheres, his ancient round:
> His path predestined through Creation
> He ends with step of thunder-sound.
> The angels from his visage splendid
> Draw power, whose measure none can say;
> The lofty works, uncomprehended,
> Are bright as on the earliest day.

Gabriel evokes the terrifying dynamism of the universe: the incomprehensible speed of its processes, and above all the swift, rhythmical changes of day and night. (The alternating play of light and dark* marks the whole

---

* One is repeatedly reminded of Goethe's long interest in light and color. An "eye-person" (*Augenmensch*), he was fascinated by all aspects of seeing.

FAUST I: THE LITTLE WORLD

poem.) Then Michael "heightens" Gabriel's statement by stressing the destructive forces of nature, but ends:

> Yet, Lord, Thy messengers are praising
> The gentle movement of Thy day.

Under the aspect of eternity, even the wildest tempests appear as parts of a divinely ordained plan, hence "gentle." In a brief reprise, the angels vary this thought: the angels draw strength from the spectacle *because* it is incomprehensible.

Enter Mephisto—darkness after light—and the whole tone changes. Unlike the angels, he remarks with his usual sarcasm, he can utter no "lofty words"; he has nothing to say about astronomical glories, being concerned with man. Man's condition is the most parlous of all; misusing the god-given "appearance of heavenly light," man behaves more bestially than any beast. God throws the name of Faust into the argument; he appears in Mephisto's sharp but not inaccurate portrayal as an idealist and enthusiast, utterly incapable of finding satisfaction. In reply the Lord uses Goethe's favorite image of organic growth: the tree will bring forth blossoms and fruit, Faust will "soon" be led to clarity, to light. Mephisto offers to wager that he can seduce Faust; obviously, the Almighty does not take bets, but he gives Mephisto a free hand as long as Faust's life lasts on this earth—the Job motif. The Lord's famous assertion that man errs as long as he strives has been much debated and often misunderstood. While it does not suggest that error is good in itself, it does imply that error is inseparable fom activity, as friction is from motion; if Faust ceased to err, he would be essentially dead. (As Gillies notes, striving is not the only way to salvation presented in the poem, but it is Faust's way.)

Of course, it is very stupid of Mephisto to want to wager against Omniscience. Indeed, while he is witty, incisive, and often right at a particular moment, this devil is always mistaken about things as a whole. Actually, it is wrong to worry too much about the exact terms of either the implied wager or the ensuing pact. They are dramatic devices, propulsion units, as it were, to help the great poem get under way. "Prologue in Heaven" combines seriousness about the workings of the universe with good-natured irony in its presentation of a traditional Lord. God appears very genial, tolerating Mephisto not merely because he stirs up man, gadfly-like, but because he is a "rogue," an amusing fellow.* And after the Lord has spoken a sublime farewell to His angels—secure within the "gentle bounds of love," they are to impose form on the inchoate mass of becoming—Mephisto, typically, closes the scene with a wisecrack.

In the ensuing scene, "Night," the tragedy proper begins. Faust appears in his study, that famous "high-arched, narrow Gothic room." The verse form is now that of irregular four-beat lines, variously rhymed, which Goethe took over from Hans Sachs. The first of Faust's several long monologues shows him to be labile, dissatisfied of course, idealistic but self-centered, tremendously ambi-

* On one occasion, Goethe even spoke (half-seriously?) of saving Mephisto.

FAUST I: THE LITTLE WORLD

tious, and profoundly romantic. Beginning with the traditional "survey of the faculties," the monologue states the insufficiency of the four disciplines—including "alas, theology"—and the vanity of academic glory. At once it must be stressed that he is not the sinister mage of tradition, lusting after power, or after knowledge as a means to power. In Faust, Promethean striving and Werther-like sensitivity are uneasily yoked together; small wonder that he is mercurial. Part of his very real despair stems from the frustration of his wish "to better people and change their lives." Yet at this point in his life Faust has no friends, no equals; his affection for mankind is revealingly abstract. By turning to magic, he hopes to discover the real, seminal powers which move the world, abandoning "huckstering in words." It is a laudable ambition, incidentally typical of the Storm-and-Stress movement. (Faust's revolt against empty, "scholastic" knowledge is not anti-intellectual; quite the reverse.) A typically Goethean glimpse of the moon suggests a flight into nature and makes his musty "prison," his study, seem all the more unbearable. Academic learning is the realm of death —"animal skeletons and dead bones"—and darkness. To live, he must flee into "open country." In a book of Nostradamus, he finds the sign of the macrocosm, symbol of the living, ordered universe. At first he is exalted:

> Am I a god? All becomes clearer to me!
> I see in these pure lines
> creative nature lying open before my soul.

But with a sudden, characteristic reversal of feeling, he realizes that this is only a "spectacle"—presumably the symbol is too lofty to have direct emotional significance. To find the true sources of life, the breasts of nature, he must look elsewhere.

Turning the pages of the magical book, he sees the sign of the Earth Spirit—presumably the concretion of the physical forces of the universe, birth and death, procreation and destruction, the Lucretian Mars and Venus, as Santayana put it. Tangible, earthy reality is precisely what Faust is seeking: he senses a glow of courage, of *élan vital*. Yet when the spirit he has summoned appears in a flame, he is terrified. With heavy sarcasm, the spirit mocks him: the would-be superman is a miserable worm. Stung to rashness, Faust claims that he is closely linked to the spirit, only to be shattered by the reply:

> You are like the spirit you comprehend,
> Not me.

And the spirit vanishes. Not for the last time, Faust is deceived by his own subjectivity, a type of unconscious arrogance not uncommon in intellectuals.

Faust's despair is interrupted by the knock of his "famulus" or assistant, Wagner. Not a bad fellow, poor Wagner has become the symbol of the utter pedant. To be sure, he is industrious, eager for knowledge, loyal to his master; when we meet him again, in Part II, he has reached the top of the academic ladder. Actually he is a sort of parody of Faust; this is especially clear in the delicious line which closes this scene: "Yes, I know much, but want to know it all." Wagner is never seriously tempted to leave the academy. In view of his career, one

FAUST I: THE LITTLE WORLD

feels that Faust was justified in signing the pact, for if he had stayed on in an environment he loathed, increasingly filled with self-disgust, he would truly have sold his soul. The dialogue between the two contrasts Faust's belief in sincere feeling to Wagner's pathetic hope of finding in oratory a short cut to success, Wagner's simple faith in progress to Faust's radical skepticism. Since we cannot comprehend the past, let alone judge it, notions of human betterment are simply irrelevant; the student's clichés are impatiently brushed aside:

> the ages that are past
> Are now a book with seven seals protected:
> What you the spirit of the ages call
> Is nothing but the spirit of you all,
> Wherein the ages are reflected.

If Mephisto reflects the Voltairean wit and brilliance of the Enlightenment, Wagner mirrors its duller side; he is the plodding, simple-minded *Aufklärer* whom the new generation delighted to ridicule.

Once the famulus departs, Faust is again free to wrestle with the problem of his existence. In a second long monologue, he rehearses his defeat by the Earth Spirit: he, "more than cherub," a man in God's image, has felt himself a dwarf, a worm—that insult has stuck in his memory. Yet he can speak of the moment just before his rejection as blessed; it was an instant of self-transcendence in which he felt himself great—and simultaneously small. His thoughts stray to the theme of care—of obsessive, self-destroying worry, and he gives a brilliantly concise image of a neurotic state:

> We dread the blows we never feel,
> And what we never lose is yet by us lamented!

Like Werther, Faust has a real flair for self-analysis. Here it serves as a skillful anticipation of the theme of suicide. (One recalls Goethe's warning against trying to gain self-knowledge through introspection.) The word "worm" makes Faust think of dust: the association runs to his dusty surroundings, to the obsolete apparatus in his study, which will not serve as a key to the secrets of the universe. His glance falls on a vial of poison; suddenly he launches into an ecstatic glorification of death. Since study and magic have failed him, what remains? Death appears as a shining sea, and "A new day summons me toward a new shore." With a shift of metaphor as swift as that in Tasso's last speech, Faust envisions a chariot of fire to bear him upward to "new spheres" of action. Like Werther, he is entranced by the thought of flying. (The image, often repeated, unobtrusively underscores his "soaring" nature.) Brushing away fears of Hell as superstitious, he convinces himself—momentarily—that his death will prove his heroic courage. Concluding a speech of eloquent bravado, he raises a poison-filled goblet to his lips.

Just then there is a peal of bells, and a chorus proclaiming the Resurrection is heard (Wagner casually mentioned that it was the eve of Easter). The short, rhymed lines—typical of the many choruses in *Faust*—end tri-

FAUST I: THE LITTLE WORLD

umphantly. Faust is moved—not by the content of the hymn—"I hear your message, yes; yet I cannot believe"—but by the associations it has for him. His life is saved, but now a third avenue to reality, to "the absolute," has been blocked. Essentially, his condition is worse than at the beginning of the drama—a further reason for Mephisto (who has been spying on Faust) to be hopeful of success.

"Before the Gate," set on Easter Day, is a scene which shifts us back to the light again. Admirably vernal and gay, it is informed by a secularized Easter spirit: the citizens of the walled town where Faust lives rejoice in the color and freshness of the countryside. As he puts it, they celebrate the Resurrection because they have themselves risen from the cramped cold of winter. He and Wagner, out for a walk, encounter a colorful variety of people: apprentices, Philistine burghers, girls of various classes, boys hoping for amorous adventure, and so on. The tone of the first part of the scene is one of cheerful realism. Again the technique of anticipation: the soldiers' song is erotic and also points forward to Valentine, Gretchen's martial brother; a second song, picturing a seduction, looks toward the "Gretchen tragedy." For the moment, Faust can enter into the holiday spirit; Wagner is too stiff and correct to do so.

Characteristically, Faust cannot enjoy his mood of relaxation for long. A well-meaning peasant praises him and his father for having saved many lives during a pestilent epidemic years before. Actually, he tells Wagner, they had killed far more people than the disease, with their alchemistic remedies. Instead of relapsing into melancholy, Faust again has a vision of flying; with a splendid soaring of the imagination, he sees himself on high—"The day before me, and the night behind"—and evokes the lark, the eagle with wings outstretched, the crane flying homeward. Superfluously enough, Wagner assures Faust that *he* never has such moods; enough to be borne "from book to book, from page to page." This elicits Faust's famous self-description: while Wagner is conscious of only one urgent drive, he has two souls: one directed, in earthy passion, to the things of this world; the other intellectual, lofty, sublimated. Clearly, this is no sign of a pathological "split" in Faust; in his complexity he is more fully realized, more truly human than Wagner, but for that reason his life is more difficult. Rhetorically, he invokes "spirits in the air, if such there are," repeating the motif of flight and frightening Wagner, who has a superstitious strain behind his rationalistic façade. More importantly, the mention of spirits anticipates the entrance of Mephisto, who now appears in the guise of a black poodle, encircling the pair and leaving fiery circles behind him. Faust senses the approach of the supernatural, while Wagner is comfortably sure that it is merely a friendly creature. One of his redeeming traits is his fondness for dogs.

The next scene, set in Faust's study, shows yet another aspect of Faust's personality. For the moment, his "better soul"—that part of his nature which aspires to high intellectual achievement—is in command; his mood is tranquil:

> The love of man revives within us,
> The love of God revives again.

FAUST I: THE LITTLE WORLD

Naturally, Mephisto does not approve: the poodle begins to growl. After its second interruption, Faust turns to the New Testament; if inspiration falters, it can be renewed in revelation. Turning to the Book of John, he begins to translate from the Greek—briefly, one associates him with Luther. While not a believer, Faust has a religious vein; he is "un-Christian though not anti-Christian"; he can feel reverence for the Bible, as for nature. The translation, which never gets beyond the first sentence "In the beginning was the Word"—reveals his full impatience and arbitrariness. Taking *word* literally, as a mere lifeless sign, he rejects it: nor will *thought* or *intention* serve. Like a good Storm-and-Stress enthusiast, he hits upon *force* or *energy*, but finally writes triumphantly "In the beginning was the *deed*." Obviously, he has committed a sort of intellectual rape, and the line could serve as a slogan for any amount of mindless activism. Apparently the poodle does not realize how impious Faust's translation is; to sabotage it, the dog barks, howls, and finally swells up like a cloud and assumes the form of a hippopotamus. By no means intimidated, Faust tries first secular and then Christian magic; threatened by the symbol of the Trinity, Mephisto steps out of the dissolving vapor, dressed as a traveling scholar. Faust, who is in fine fettle throughout and far superior to his antagonist, remarks: "So *that* then was the poodle's core!"

After some dialectical fencing, Mephisto defines his nature and duties. (He refuses to give his name, but Faust has sensed immediately who his guest is.) When Mephisto describes himself as the spirit of perpetual denial, he is completely in earnest:

> for all things, from the void
> Called forth, deserve to be destroyed....

His reference to the Manichaean conflict between darkness and light reiterates this key image of the poem. Too acute to believe in a complete victory over the forces of procreation, he identifies himself with fire—the one element free of the germs of life—and continues his futile campaign. From the Lord's point of view, which is essentially that of the poem, Mephisto's activities are a part of the plan of the world; he is the gadfly, we recall, the unconscious instrument of the good, and, paradoxically, of Faust's ultimate salvation. (One has the right to find this optimism excessive, or to be vexed by it, as was Santayana's Oliver Alden; but it is in the poem.) Faust at once sees the impossibility of Mephisto's struggle against Omnipotence, and advises the "eccentric son of chaos" to try another line of work.

Some "magical" stage-business is used as a bridge to the famous pact. Upon learning that Mephisto cannot leave without his permission, being inhibited by a magic sign and infernal laws, Faust remarks that if devils are themselves bound by a system of law, one could "sign a pact with you gentlemen." His tone is ironic, *de haut en bas;* fearing "neither Hell nor devil" nor the loss of his soul, he is ready for an adventure which at the moment he does not take seriously. In part though, he has underrated his adversary; Mephisto summons a chorus of spirits—we have already heard them singing or chanting in the corridor—to lull Faust to sleep. Their song, in its short dactylic lines, formally recalls the Easter hymn;

FAUST I: THE LITTLE WORLD

but its burden is pagan. It conjures up an idyllic, Mediterranean landscape, where "milder suns" illuminate scenes of love and wine. Skillfully, Mephisto has appealed to a long-repressed side of Faust; the honors are now even. When Faust awakes, he wonders if it has not been all a dream.

The next scene, also set in the study, is more important in what it tells us about Faust than in its statement of the terms of the pact. Dressed as a young nobleman this time, Mephisto appears, blandly proposing to take Faust on a sort of grand tour, where he can really learn "what life is." The superficiality of this suggestion infuriates Faust: he hopes for nothing from the world; he is "Too old . . . to play with passion; / Too young, to be without desire." Life is a matter of deprivation and frustration. Every day brings disappointment, every night its terrifying dreams. Above all, he cannot realize his inner powers —"the god within"—in authentic activity. Life is hateful; again he states his wish to die.

When Mephisto taunts him with his failure to commit suicide, Faust's despair is "heightened" to a total rejection of existence, culminating in his cursing the Christian virtues: love, hope, faith, and "patience, above all." This mood of existential denial corresponds in its way to Mephisto's nihilism, though this rather limited devil cannot really grasp it. A chorus of invisible spirits laments that Faust has "destroyed / The lovely world" and urges him to rebuild it more splendidly by beginning a new life. It is the familiar Goethean theme of death and renewal. From the immediate point of view, the spirits further Mephisto's plans and are evil; from that of the total poem, they are beneficent, like the spirits who restore Faust after Gretchen's death. At any rate, he is diverted from black despair. Mephisto offers to be his servant during his life on earth; "over there," the roles will be reversed. Thoroughly "this-worldly," Faust declares that life on earth is what matters. (Again, he does not deny the possibility of other "spheres" of being, but finds them irrelevant.) Mockingly, he lists the gifts which such a "poor devil" might provide: evanescent gold, faithless love, and so on. Missing the sarcasm, Mephisto claims that he can procure all that and more: comfortable repose—the last thing that could attract Faust. In reply, he scornfuly offers the wager in its first formulation. If he ever rests upon a bed of ease, ever becomes self-satisfied, ever is taken in by the pleasures Mephisto procures, let that day be his last.

Mephisto at once agrees, and Faust rushes ahead, restating the bet with a significant variation:

> If ever I say to any moment:
> 'Linger—you are so wonderful!'
> Then you may throw me in chains.
> I'll be ready for the earth.

As the wager is now phrased, Faust will lose if he asks that any moment of experience whatsoever be prolonged; it is no longer merely a matter of remaining indifferent to the meretricious delights a "poor devil" can offer. Also, focusing our attention on a single crucial point—that the moment be prolonged—adds greatly to the dramatic tension. (Almost at the end of the poem, Faust does utter

FAUST I: THE LITTLE WORLD

the fateful words, but with a significant modification). Breaking the accepted legendary pattern, Goethe does not have his hero "sell his soul." Rather, he "bets his life"—and by implication, his soul in the hereafter—that he will remain dynamically unsatisfied. Since Faust does not believe in a traditional heaven or hell, he is not risking much. From one point of view, one can sympathize with Mephisto's later belief that he has been cheated. Above all, Faust is betting that he will remain himself—restless in his divine discontent—an active, striving monad or entelechy. Under the aspect of the "Prologue in Heaven," he cannot possibly lose. In fact, the terms of the wager are not consistently enforced: once Faust has found Helen, he clearly wants the "fair moment" to be made permanent (see page 204). Thus while the wager is extremely important as a dramatic device, it is not in itself decisive.

In part, Faust makes his agreement out of despair, influenced, as he says, by the Earth Spirit's rejection. At first, the wager (or compact, as he later calls it after signing his name in blood, in the traditional manner), is profoundly nihilistic: on the one hand, empty pleasures of earth; on the other, empty threats of hell. He is offering to trade nothing for nothing. But almost at once Faust's true intention becomes clear: he will *use* Mephisto and the wager as the means of finding total experience.

> I mean to enjoy
> in my innermost being all that is offered to mankind,
> to seize the highest and the lowest,
> to mix all kinds of good and evil,

and thus expand my Self till it includes
the spirit of all men—

Rational knowledge and magic having failed, experience alone remains as the road to authentic reality. Perhaps totality can be reached by accumulating an infinite number of single experiences. Faust's goal would appear to be that of the Renaissance "universal man," but set in emotional rather than intellectual terms. The ideal of universality Goethe stated much less romantically in a gnomic couplet: "If you want to stride into the infinite / Just go, in the finite, in every direction." Of course Faust's assault on the absolute is less rational, more impulsive. Yet what he wants is not intrinsically evil; from the point of view of the Lord, it is basically good: Faust's striving will eventually bring "clarity"; he will run his destined course. On the way, through subjectivity, rashness, and occasional *hubris* he will do evil things, but they are allowed for in the generous calculations of Heaven: "Man errs as long as his striving lasts."

In a sense, then, Faust has already found the beginning of the right path; he has at least escaped from self-consuming frustration. Before he proceeds very far, he will cause tragedy and ruin. His career will be long and tortuous, but only an instant, after all, in the vast pageant which the Lord and His angels survey.

In his excellent *Goethe's Major Plays*, Ronald Peacock points out that Faust's ambition appears from this point on more human, less magical; life itself, as life, is the goal, an idea which had occurred to none of his mythical predecessors. This is true, and important. To make life

FAUST I: THE LITTLE WORLD

as such an absolute, answerable to no human or divine judge, would invite moral anarchy. The poem does not do so, but still less does it condemn Faust's cult of total experience as utterly wrong. It is a first step in the activist's long progress, an advance at least beyond suicidal despair or complete reliance on "magic."

To return to the text: Mephisto's hopes are now naturally high, especially when he hears Faust's words about "quenching glowing passions / In the depths of sensuality." For the protagonist's more titanic aspirations he has a common-sense answer: only a god can comprehend the whole of existence; man is subject to the alternations of his dual nature, to "day and night." Even vicariously, through poetry, one cannot really become a microcosm; one is what one is. It is high time to leave these barren speculations, he urges, for the tangible joys of sensuality, which lie around us like green pastures.

While Faust has mental reservations, as we know, he is eager to set out on his adventures. An inopportune visitor intervenes, a young student, eager to gain the advice and favor of the famous scholar. In his present state of mind, Faust cannot bear to see the boy; Mephisto is all too glad to put on Faust's academic robe and play faculty adviser. In a scene rich in parody, he gives a second survey of the curriculum, an infernal variation on Faust's first lines. Logic, metaphysics, theology are all scored; medicine is another matter, since it gives the physician such opportunities to seduce his patients. When the devil contrasts "gray theory" to the "green and golden tree of life," we are again reminded of Faust's protests against sterile abstractions. This devil can quote Storm and Stress slogans for his own purpose. His famous praise of new experience over all theory reminds one of Faust's phrase "feeling is all"; of course it is not the poem's last word on the matter. With really infernal cynicism, Mephisto writes a line from Genesis in the student's album: "You shall be like God, knowing good and evil." Perhaps this miniature Faust* can also be led to eat forbidden fruit. Bewildered, the student leaves; Faust reappears; Mephisto promises to show him first "the small, then the great world"—the bourgeois German sphere of the First, and the imperial scope of the Second Part.

Gradually one becomes aware that the bond between Mephisto and Faust is uncannily close. On one level, as various commentators have observed, he is the negative element in Faust, his sinister double or "shadow." When treating Faust as a dramatic poem, however, it seems best to keep the two figures separate. In his comments on academic subjects, and particularly in his repartee with Faust, Mephisto is often right. At times he punctures Faust's inflated delusions with a word. When for example he remarks in an aside that if Faust will just keep on with his anti-intellectualism, his scorn of reason and knowledge, he will surely be lost, one feels that Goethe (and the poem) agree with him. Again, Mephisto is generally right about specific matters, and even, as Santayana says, delightful; but his vision is narrow, his image of Faust is inadequate, and he is woefully wrong in his tactics and his total strategy. While he wins some battles, he loses the war.

* He reappears as the Bachelor of Arts in Part II; see page 188.

FAUST I: THE LITTLE WORLD

Mephisto starts his campaign very modestly, by introducing Faust into a society of dissipated students in the scene "Auerbach's Cellar." Finding them less than amusing, he can hardly hope that their inane revels will satisfy his antagonist. Perhaps he deliberately begins on a low pitch, intending to lead Faust gradually to a climax of temptation. Probably, however, Goethe included the scene because it is a traditional part of the legend—he had visited the actual "Auerbach's Cellar," with its pictures of the magician's pranks, while a student at Leipzig—and because it furnished the raw material for a scene of broad comedy. In any event, the poem itself follows the familiar pattern of "heightening" in its depiction of ugliness as in other ways: it moves from these rather dull brawlers through the grotesqueness of "Witch's Kitchen" to the truly infernal dissipations of "Walpurgis Night." (That Goethe includes satiric political sallies in all these scenes tells us a good deal about his attitude. Here it is a drunk who shouts: "Long live freedom!")

The scene opens with a genre picture of the four students; the stage direction calls them "merry fellows" ironically, for they are actually bored and bitter. Not yet sufficiently alcoholized to escape from their own selves, they try to induce gaiety first by a crude practical joke, then by singing a song, "There was a rat in the cellar-hole," which combines an account of the animal's death with a nasty sexuality. Beast images prevail: besides the rat, swine, sows, a he-goat, and a flea occur. This sordidness is reinforced by the two cellars (the scene itself and that in the song) and by mentioning the Blocksberg, where witches celebrate their obscene rites annually. To

155

bring life into the proceedings, Mephisto teases the students, sings his famous song about the flea, and makes his victims believe that each is drinking the wine of his choice. When the wine turns out to be fire and the frightened dupes seek revenge, he puts them under another spell and escapes with Faust.

Perhaps the best line in the scene is Faust's: "I would be glad to leave them now." Far from being entranced, he is actively bored. And the popularity of the scene is perhaps due less to comic relief—it is not very funny—than to its use of music and startling stage effects: the wine suddenly bursting into flames, and so on. As Beutler has remarked, its theatrical strength lies not in the noisy foolishness, but in the chance it gives Mephisto to prove his daemonic power by inspiring "primitive uncanny terror" in the students.

In the ensuing scene, "Witch's Kitchen," Faust's mood is still one of disgust. Mephisto has brought him to this grotesque room so that he may be magically rejuvenated. Significantly, animals—a family of apes—and fire—the devil's element—again dominate the stage. It is the second successive "dark" incident, blacker than "Auerbach's Cellar." Light will have its turn only when Gretchen appears.

Why must Faust be rejuvenated at all? Obviously, he is not senile: the passionate vigor of his early monologues makes that clear, and in the sordid "kitchen" itself he is attracted by the image of a lovely woman in the magic mirror *before* he drinks the aphrodisiac the witch has brewed. In combination, two suggestions help to supply an answer: the potion does not cause, but accelerates, his

FAUST I: THE LITTLE WORLD

erotic drive; Goethe, with his belief in metamorphosis, wished to emphasize the theme of renewal.

Pointing forward to "Walpurgis Night" in its mingling of magic, lust, ugliness, and wit, "Witch's Kitchen" is largely centered on evil or "black" eroticism. At the same time, the recumbent nude figure Faust sees in the mirror seems linked to classical, "healthy" sexuality; hers is the only beauty in the scene. While she is not Helen or any specific woman, her image anticipates Faust's later visions of Leda and the Swan. Perhaps Goethe had a picture of Titian's or Giorgione's in mind. Faust's reaction is romantic, in contrast to the cynicism of his companion:

> And must I see in this reclining body
> The inner sense of every paradise?

When he adds—

> Can such a thing exist on earth?—

we note that he has indeed led an academic existence.

As the action opens, Faust stresses his aversion to rejuvenation by black magic at the hands of an "old woman," but inevitably rejects Mephisto's sarcastic suggestion that he live the "simple life" of a peasant. "And so the witch will have to serve." The apes, with their rudeness and their satiric comment on contemporary follies, add a fittingly bestial note. (They speak in short, rhymed, often enigmatic lines; those of the rest of the scene follow mainly the familiar four- or five-stress pattern). Throughout, the attitude toward black magic is ambivalent: it is repulsive, practiced by charlatans, and nevertheless effective. The Witch, ill-tempered, nasty, but with a certain slatternly force, is admirably drawn. As for Mephisto, he is at his most infernal and most witty. Ordering a draft of the stinking aphrodisiac for Faust, he tells the Witch: "And pour him out a nice full cup." We might be at a bourgeois *Kaffeeklatsch*. He calls her "admirable Sibyl"—elsewhere, as a Nordic devil, he remains at a far remove from the classical world. Naturally, he is in high spirits: he has the upper hand, and keeps it until the "peripety" during the Walpurgis Night.

Despite his repugnance and his glimpse of authentic beauty, Faust does drink the potion; a slender flame, the devil's element, rises from the potentially lethal brew. As Gillies notes, Faust—at least in this part of the poem—is continually expressing his scruples and his higher nature and then proceeding to do what his lower nature demands. It is a very human trait but not an endearing one. From his reaction, there is no doubt that the potion is effective. Closing the scene, Mephisto comments that with such a drink inside him, he will see a Helen of Troy in every woman he meets. It is hardly a happy portent for the one he actually encounters.

In fact, the next line of the poem, which opens the scene "Street," shows him addressing Gretchen,* with the practiced boldness of a roué, as "lovely lady." It is a tribute to the poignancy of the "Gretchen tragedy" that one soon forgets, as it develops, the sordid preliminaries

---

* Her name is Margarete, but Faust generally uses the diminutive, as do the commentators.

FAUST I: THE LITTLE WORLD

of "Witch's Kitchen" and must believe that Faust, however ruthless and deluded, does love Gretchen in his fashion. Not that one can absolve him of guilt by assigning most of the responsibility to Mephisto; such a "vindication" would merely reduce Faust to a puppet.

As the tragedy rapidly unfolds, we gradually descry in Gretchen, presented as she is affectionately but not sentimentally, a person of tragic stature—not a sweet, utterly innocent, merely pathetic victim. Simplicity, directness, and pertness are our first impression; she is without formal education of course, but far from stupid. Why is she so easily vulnerable to Faust's plans? Rapidly and very economically, the poem tells us: she is lonely, and she resents her mother's strictness and stinginess, which has frustrated her normal feminine fondness for pretty things. While she is essentially "pure" she is by no means sexless; like Clara in *Egmont*, she is capable of genuine passion. At the end of the poem she is to be sure grouped with "the easily seducible" but, most emphatically, she is "saved." Her maternal side, like Lotte's, is deftly emphasized. "It is not the least part of her tragedy . . . ," Peacock has observed, "that her actual fate, to bear her child in shame and drown it, is the direct opposite of her true vocation, to bear a child in happiness and be its mother."

At the same time Gretchen is, as Santayana put it, "the only true Christian in this poem." Her genuine religious sense is evident not only in her instinctive aversion to Mephisto—whom she defeats completely in the long run —nor in her intuitive insight that Faust, for all his fine phrases, "has no Christianity." It is clear above all in her acceptance of punishment, at the end of *Faust I:* she has sinned and repented, and wishes only the "judgment of God." Here she acts not from a conscious moral choice, as Schiller's heroines do, but because of the necessity of her nature. Like Mephisto, but in the opposite sense, she is one of the very few realists in *Faust.* Even when she is distraught, half-mad, she realizes that to escape with her lover, to lead the life of guilt-ridden outcasts, would be unbearable, practically as well as morally.

It has often been observed that *Faust I* consists of two disparate halves, very imperfectly integrated: the fragmentary "scholar's tragedy" and the Gretchen action, which is virtually complete in itself. In its own terms, the objection is correct. From the point of view of the total poem however, there are five main actions, set inside a cosmic frame and each centered on one dominating figure: Faust the scholar; Gretchen; then in Part II: Homunculus; Helen; Faust the colonizer. What holds them together is above all the sense of "Faustian" drive in the natural world as well as in the protagonist himself.

Thirteen scenes, most of them quite short, contain the account of Gretchen's love, guilt, and despair. The scene "Forest and Cavern," showing Faust's belated attempt to break away before he must "ruin" Gretchen, briefly shifts the focus away from her. After her collapse in the scene "Cathedral," comes the long episode—no *mere* episode, of course—of Walpurgis Night; two brief scenes showing Faust's return, with Mephisto, to rescue his beloved, now sentenced to death for infanticide; and her moral triumph in the final scene, "Prison." In speaking of Gretchen's love, guilt, and despair, I have not forgotten Faust's. But it is she, after all, for whom we feel pity and fear; he plays, to put it mildly, no admirable role. Not that he is ever a black villain; he "means well," has hesitations and doubts, behaves "naturally." Nor would the most naive reader expect him to "marry and settle down." From the point of view of the poem, he too acts under the stress of necessity—call it biological necessity perhaps. But even if one accepts this viewpoint completely—it is very hard to—the fact remains that he suffers far less for his "inevitable" actions than she for hers. To be sure, he is punished: he feels guilt and remorse, and must experience utter rejection when Gretchen, for a moment, turns away from him in horror and fear. Then the Second Part shows him recovered, purged of remorse. This is no moralistic reproach to the poem, or to Goethe, merely an argument that it is *her* tragedy.

The eight scenes preceding the crucial "Forest and Cavern" are relatively bright though we sense at once that this love will have no happy outcome; the five after Faust's return are almost entirely dark. Besides this basic alternation there are other, and brilliant, contrast effects. Thus "Evening" shows us first Faust's sentimental raptures in Gretchen's room (Mephisto has smuggled him in and left a casket of jewels there, the first important step in the campaign of seduction) and then Gretchen's song of authentic fidelity in love, "The King in Thule," which tells us at least as much about her as any direct exposition could. In the ensuing scene, Mephisto's disgust on learning that the Church has gotten hold of the jewels affords a comic counterpoint to the melancholy of Gretchen's song. (His remark about the Church's robust stomach for ill-gotten goods anticipates Eliot's early line: "The Church can sleep and feed at once.") Similarly, Gretchen's innocence is set off against the grossness of her neighbor Frau Martha Schwerdtlein, that low-comedy figure, grass widow, and amateur procuress, whose house is used for the lovers' early meetings; Gretchen's fidelity is balanced against Martha's eagerness to marry again, once she is sure that her husband is legally and officially dead. In the beautifully constructed scene "Garden" two couples alternate on the stage: the lovers, and Martha and Mephisto; the widow's amorous advances frighten even the devil.

Probably the greatest contrasts lie in the clashes between Faust and Mephisto and Faust and Faust.* When the devil's cynical realism is opposed to the protagonist's sentimental self-delusion, it is usually the latter which seems more dangerous. This emerges most vividly in the debate between the two involving eternity and the transitoriness of passion. To Mephisto's taunts that Faust will overcome Gretchen's scruples with empty words "about eternal faith and love," he replies with a rhetorical question: when he claims that the emotion he feels, his "glow," is eternal, can that be a lie? And a bit later, to Gretchen, he uses the word "eternal" twice; he is not consciously lying, but trying to persuade himself that his emotion is sacred. (To win the wager, Mephisto should try to convince Faust that he has found a lasting, and hence of course satisfying "moment"; but the details of

* In a sense the two conflicts are both fought out within Faust; see page 154.

FAUST I: THE LITTLE WORLD

their agreement, fortunately, are already fading into the background.) In the long run Faust's love is vindicated; but in the immediate, concrete situation, Mephisto's view is far more accurate. As so often, both are right and both are wrong. And while Faust, at the time when he is psychologically closest to Gretchen, seems ready to break with the devil, whom he calls "a beast," he is still far from being strong enough to cut the scarlet cord which binds him to his worser self.

The conflict "Faust versus Faust" appears most clearly in those periods of self-reproach when he considers leaving Gretchen before it is "too late." Such moods persist almost until the moment of actual seduction; they are not insincere, but one cannot take them too seriously. His concluding line, after the discussion about the "eternity" of passion, is unexpectedly realistic: "For you [Mephisto] are right, especially since I must."

In the "Gretchen action" the symbolic images are appropriately simple, and are used economically and unobtrusively. When Gretchen plucks the petals from a flower, we may anticipate her "fall," remembering the poem "Wild Rose" (see p. 26). After it has taken place, her brother bitterly notes that she was once known as the blossom of all girls. Soon after she has sung of a golden goblet, she discovers the casket with its golden ornaments and jewels; then comes her wry statement that everyone clings to gold and depends upon it. Often passion is expressed in images of flame and "glowing"; but it may equally be symbolized as a brook or an Alpine cataract.

In "Forest and Cavern" Faust has left the "small, medieval Imperial city" where Gretchen lives, hoping to draw from nature the strength and calm to overcome his passion. At first it appears that he is succeeding: in a lovely, serene monologue set in blank verse, he thanks the "spirit sublime" who has given him all he asked for: intuitive, warm insight into nature, self-knowledge, memories of a beautiful past, and "the austere delight of thought." Obviously, his "higher soul" is in command again; this is the mood in which he began to translate the Gospel of John.

When we read that the benevolent "spirit sublime" had appeared to Faust in the fire, we are startled; for obviously, he must refer to the Earth Spirit, who had treated him with crushing scorn. One can only say that Faust now sees nature with very different eyes.* But alas, man cannot find perfection: even the now beneficent Earth Spirit has sent the companion "whom I can no longer do without." Thus announced, Mephisto enters to resume his work of sabotage. After a brisk exchange of insults with his charge, he comes to the point: Gretchen is pining away, believing that she has been deserted. Here his cleverness is really infernal, for Faust has indeed already wronged her, having seduced her morally and left her alone. Sophistical though the implication is: "You might as well wrong her completely, now," Faust's exclamation "Serpent, serpent" is testimony to the keenness

* This is one of the inconsistencies of the poem which no "unitarian" ingenuity can smooth away, for nothing in the text gives any preparation for the startling change. Similarly, the reference to Earth Spirit's sending Mephisto to Faust goes back to an earlier plan; also, the scene was originally planned to come after Gretchen's seduction. But if the details are confused, the general import of "Forest and Cavern" is clear, and its importance great.

FAUST I: THE LITTLE WORLD

of the thrust, and he confesses that he is half-crazed with desire for "her sweet body." With desperate eloquence, he compares himself to a raging torrent which has destroyed the idyllic "little world" of Gretchen's existence. He capitulates; come what may, he will return, even though both of them be destroyed. Again, he uses the word "must" to express the compulsion he feels. In fact, his earlier admission that he can no longer do without the devil has shown what his decision will be. Neither "nature" nor Spinozan contemplation can overcome passion once it is aroused—not in Faust's case at least. As so often, Mephisto's sarcastic comment is true as far as it goes: since Faust is going to act diabolically, he should at least not play the role of a devil with a bad conscience.

Gretchen, meanwhile, is even more at the mercy of necessity than is Faust. Her monologue at the spinning wheel is also spoken during the time of separation; it balances Faust's address to the "spirit sublime" and, in its lyric simplicity, forms a sharp contrast to his rhetoric. Accepting her love, she does not try to evade or deny it. Three times she repeats the brief verse beginning "My peace is gone." She too expresses the power of her desire, she too is willing to die if it may be consummated. But it would be impossible for her to speak or to conceive, as Faust does, of the destruction of her lover.

The climax of passion is reached in the next scene, ominously if inevitably set in Martha's garden. Loving Faust without reservation, deeply disturbed by his association with Mephisto, she asks him directly if he believes in God. He replies with an eloquent confession of pantheistic (or panentheistic) faith. Nature, life itself, his existence and hers, inspire a sense of bliss which can be called happiness, the heart, love, or God:

Feeling is all.*
The name is sound and smoke,
Beclouding Heaven's glow.

Clearly, Faust is not lying about his beliefs; clearly also his impassioned words evade a direct answer to her question, and thus are intended to remove a possible barrier between Gretchen and himself. Only half satisfied, she continues to speak of her aversion to Mephisto; finally, as she is about to leave, he asks her if they may not become lovers. So that they may be undisturbed when he comes to her room, he gives her a sleeping draught for her mother.

From this point, the poem develops the tragedy with frightening speed. In the next scene, "At the Fountain," Gretchen learns from the viciously moralistic Lisbeth that an acquaintaince of theirs has become pregnant. Her lover has fled; even if he should finally marry her, she will be publicly disgraced. Like Gretchen, we feel that her own downfall is now certain. How much poetic time has passed, we do not know, but by the time-scale of the reader, the first intimation of catastrophe follows immediately upon the night of love.

The sense of impending disaster is heightened in Gretchen's ensuing monologue. She has brought flowers to offer at the shrine of the Mater Dolorosa, whose statue stands in a niche of the city wall. In lines combining

---

* See above, p. 2f.

FAUST I: THE LITTLE WORLD

motifs from the hymn "Stabat mater" and other medieval Latin poetry, she pours out her desperation. She too feels "the sword in the heart"; in a bitter, all too literal sense, she too is a *mater dolorosa*. Some months have passed; Faust has obviously deserted her. (Significantly, he is mentioned neither in this nor the preceding scene.) Her final prayer, imploring the Virgin to save her from "disgrace and death" may indicate that her mother has already died after taking too much of the sleeping potion; more probably it is an intuitive anticipation of things to come. That we never see her mother somewhat mutes the horror of the slaughter, one by one, of Gretchen's family, and to that extent diverts us from Faust's guilt.

That guilt is glaringly evident in "Night," in which the protagonist is seen in his least impressive stage, almost completely subject to Mephisto. After his unexplained absence from our view—we do not know where he has been or how long it is since he has seen Gretchen[*]— Faust, accompanied by Mephisto, is about to visit her. First however comes the monologue of her brother Valentine, contrasting his former pride in Gretchen with his shame at her present reputation. The unhappy end of this brave soldier, murdered by Faust and Mephisto, has obscured the fact that he is brutal, cruel, and hopelessly conventional. While Gretchen was the "finest girl in

---

[*] Apparently, many details are deliberately left vague. Superbly realistic in its essentials, the "Gretchen tragedy" is not after all naturalistic. It seems irrelevant to ask questions like: "Just how long did the love affair last?", "Did Faust spend more than one night with Gretchen?", etc. Worse, such questions distract our view from the poem itself.

town," he loved her; now he does not hesitate to add to her ruin by denouncing her publicly.

Throughout the scene, images suggesting darkness, eeriness, and superstition emphasize the sinister nature of the action, pointing forward also to the orgies of Walpurgis Night. Thus Faust says that his heart is "nightlike"; Mephisto, thoroughly enjoying the adventure, compares himself to a tomcat on the prowl. Dim, uncanny lights shine through the gloom: the gleam of the eternal light in a nearby church, the magic glow of a buried treasure rising to the surface. Most nocturnal of all is the moral tone; when Mephisto sings a song, insulting in this context, under Gretchen's window, Faust makes no objection; and he is very willing to accept infernal aid in the fight which develops when Valentine interrupts the serenade. After Faust and Mephisto have fled, Valentine, mortally wounded, surrounded by an eager crowd, draws a vivid picture, for Gretchen, of what her life as a "whore" will be like. Throughout, his speech is appropriately direct, outspoken, conventional in imagery as in thought. In fact, the language of the scene is very stylized, except for the dialogue between Faust and the devil, with its iridescence of evil. When the crowd, speaking in chorus, tells Gretchen that the victim of the "duel" is "Your mother's son!" the sense of ironic bitterness is increased—all the more so, if we are to assume that her mother has recently died.

In the scene "Cathedral" Gretchen's sufferings reach a new intensity. Instead of the monologues spoken at her spinning wheel and before the Mater Dolorosa we are now met with the full force of the "total work of art": the

FAUST I: THE LITTLE WORLD

solemn atmosphere of the church, the peals of the organ, and finally the singing of the "Day of Wrath," one of the most magnificent, and terrifying, of Latin hymns. There is a crowd of people, but Gretchen is all the more isolated; behind her, audible to her alone, stands the Evil Spirit. (To reduce this spirit to the personification of her bad conscience would sadly weaken the impact of the action.) While the spirit's reproaches are true—her mother has died, unshriven; her brother is dead; she feels the stirrings of the unborn child—it is none the less evil, for it heightens remorse while withholding hope. Wishing to forget for a moment, she hears instead the first lines of the *Dies irae,* followed by a peal of the organ. Again the organ; again she speaks of escape; again the terrifying words of the chant—"Judex ergo cum sedebit...." Cruelly, the Christian evocation of the Last Judgment reinforces her punishment. The torture continues. In his final speech, the Evil Spirit repeats the note struck by her self-righteous brother: the pure will scorn and avoid her. Gretchen faints.

After her swoon, Barker Fairley has pointed out, the poem itself swoons, descending to the nightmare world of the unconscious, the Walpurgis Night. In its fusion of darkness, magic, eroticism, and evil, the scene is one of the climaxes of *Faust:* the "power of blackness" has never been more forcefully evoked. In terms of the plot, "Walpurgis Night" leads Faust to his lowest point: climbing the mountain is a descent into Hell, for "up" can well be "down" in myth as in dream. For Mephisto, the episode represents an effort to satisfy Faust with a "moment" of sheer sexuality and satanic debauchery. His plan fails:

at the height of the orgy Faust thinks of Gretchen, and the next scene shows him fully aware of her sufferings and resolved to save her. On another level, "Walpurgis Night" shows us Faust's unconscious or partly conscious drives: the desire to experience soulless sexuality, to know the lowest and most vicious of "what has been allotted to all mankind." Symbolically at least, he does gain this experience; he is purged of this particular obsession. As if to remind us that this part of the poem too is after all semblance, "poetry" not "truth," Goethe deliberately breaks the spell by including elements of literary and political satire directed against his contemporaries. (Again we note the Weimar doctrine of "distancing." The scene was written during the poet's most "classical" years—a fact which would be almost incredible did one not know the basically antithetic, "polar" nature of his writing and thought.)

As the action begins, Faust and Mephisto are on their way to the peak of the Brocken, where the witches hold their annual convention, attended also by devils and Satan himself, on the eve of May 1. Among Mephisto's motives is the desire to keep Faust from being shocked back into reality by learning the full horror of Gretchen's situation. As at the time of Valentine's murder, we are surrounded by darkness punctuated by dim lights; a will-o'-the-wisp guides their steep ascent. Now the sense of pathological excitement, of the exhilaration of the forbidden, is heightened.

"Sound and imagery create the total effect," as has been said. The grotesque, frightening sense of the nocturnal forest is incomparably rendered:

FAUST I: THE LITTLE WORLD

> And the roots, like serpents twisted,
> Through the sand and boulders toiling,
> Fright us, weirdest links uncoiling
> To entrap us, unresisted:
> Living knots and gnarls uncanny
> Feel with polypus-antennae
> For the wanderer.

Besides actual music, we hear the storm above, the crashing of trees and moaning of boughs, the shouts of witches overhead, and above all the onomatopoeic force of the German language, powerful even when reduced by translation, as in Mephisto's description of the witches:

> They crowd and push, they roar and clatter!
> They whirl and whistle, pull and chatter.
> They shine, spurt sparks, and stink and burn!

Along with such effects, and with visual images, especially of fire, of animals like the swine and the goat, the senses of smell and touch play their part. At times deliberate ugliness reminds us of the horror of this nightmare world: "The child is stifled, the mother bursts." Yet there are moments of beauty. Goethe was particularly proud of the lines:

> How sadly the imperfect disk now rises
> Of the red moon, with its belated glow.

In its subjectivity, the image is Faustian, but the words are spoken by Mephisto. A Spanish critic wrote of the Quixotification of Sancho Panza and the Sanchofication of Don Quixote; a similar mutual influence is at work here. For all its demonism, "Walpurgis Night" has touches of sheer Goethean high spirits, as when the armada of witches, about to land, sings out its flight plan as it were: "Cover the heath, far and wide / With your swarm of witchiness!" This both gives a vivid picture of the mountain field spotted with these rambunctious hags, as if with parachutists, and "distances" the whole operation by using the one ironic abstraction "witchiness" (*Hexenheit*).

Arrived at the celebration, Faust and Mephisto first join a group of old gentlemen, introduced by the poet as objects of political and literary satire. This seems rather tame, and indeed Faust has already expressed a wish to go to the very peak of the mountain, where he has seen "glow and whirling smoke," and a crowd streaming toward Satan himself. (Actually, Goethe wrote fragments of a scene presenting the worship of Satan, including his obscenely powerful lines celebrating gold and the sexual organs as the highest goals of man, but finally excluded them from the poem.) Soon a huckster-witch appears, peddling wares—daggers, goblets once filled with poison, etc.—which have been used to carry out a variety of crimes. When she proudly proclaims that all of her jewels have served in seductions, all of her swords in treacherous killings, we are of course reminded of Gretchen and Valentine, though Faust himself does not seem to be aware of the connection. It is a nice example of Goethe's way of "mirroring" one incident or motif in another. On another level, one can read it as part of this long nightmare of Faust's, which reveals repressed guilt as well as lust.

Appropriately, the first seductress of Jewish lore, Lilith,

FAUST I: THE LITTLE WORLD

briefly appears. Since she is "the incarnation of sensuality," she may be said to have taken the place originally planned for Satan. Then Faust dances with a beautiful young witch, Mephisto with an ugly old one. In the verses which Faust and his partner sing, the sexual reference is clear but not repulsive; Mephisto and his hag are outspokenly obscene. After a brief comic interlude, we hear of Faust's first real shock: a red mouse jumps out of the mouth of the young witch with whom he is dancing. Goethe took the motif from one of his seventeenth-century sources, reinterpreted it, and used it as a symbol of sudden nausea interrupting meretricious pleasure. Mephisto dismisses the incident as trivial, but Faust now sees "a pale, fair girl" who walks slowly, as her feet are fettered; is it not Gretchen? Much worried by the sudden stirring of Faust's conscience, the devil tries to identify the apparition as Medusa, but Faust can no longer be deceived. It is Gretchen, he insists, with the unclosed eyes of one who died alone. A narrow red line around her throat points to her execution: is this Faust's long-suppressed premonition of the end which awaits her? This too Mephisto tries, unconvincingly, to explain as an attribute of Medusa; after all, Perseus cut off her head.

Swiftly, the scene fades into an intermezzo, "Walpurgis Night's Dream." As almost everyone agrees, the content of this satiric scene has no real intrinsic relation to the poem. At best, it can be justified in terms of the plot as Mephisto's effort to divert Faust from his latest vision; in terms of psychology (perhaps) as a light, mildly amusing dream that follows a nightmare; scenically, as a bright interlude between two very dark sections.

When the "Dream" fades away, *pianissimo,* we find Faust restored to vigor, determined to act to save Gretchen. Suddenly he knows the whole sorry tale of her sufferings and present imprisonment; presumably, morally awakened at last, he has extracted it from Mephisto. This is the only scene of the *Urfaust* which Goethe did not recast into verse; it has been well remarked that the realism of the prose underscores Faust's return to reality. The lapidary title, "Gloomy Day. A Field," sets the tone. When Mephisto replies to his reproaches that Gretchen was "not the first" to meet this end, Faust finds the cynicism almost unbearable. Ignoring for the moment his own guilt, he outdoes himself in Storm-and-Stress rhetoric, evoking Gretchen's misery, calling on the Earth Spirit, cursing Mephisto. The devil points out that it was Faust who had taken the initiative in forming their alliance (a distortion, in view of the "Prologue in Heaven") and tries to frighten him by speaking of avenging spirits hovering over the grave of Valentine. Nevertheless, he agrees to help Faust to rescue Gretchen, but only in a sharply limited way. They prepare to return, on magic steeds.

In six free-verse lines, "Night. Open Field" shows Faust and Mephisto thundering past a raven-stone (a place of execution) on their black horses. Spirits surround the sinister spot; whether or not they are evil, they contribute greatly to the weird and threatening atmosphere, as do the insistent beat of the lines and the mystifying, uncanny diction. One recalls *Macbeth,* the Gypsy scene in *Götz,* and Delacroix's powerful illustration, which Goethe himself praised.

The final scene, "Prison," also takes place at night,

FAUST I: THE LITTLE WORLD

though toward the end a gray dawn is rising. Faust appears chastened, to be sure, but his belief that he can now restore the situation by rescuing Gretchen shows how far he still is from understanding her. While his words are sincere enough, they tend to be conventional and often seem rhetorical compared to hers. She is "distraught and clairvoyant" at the same time, expressing her insights in symbols. As in "Martha's Garden," the difference between them comes out vividly in the poetic quality of their speech: Gretchen generally expressing herself in short, poignant lines, though in no fixed pattern; the form varies with the rise and fall of her emotion.

As Faust, overcoming his fear, is about to unlock the door to the prison, he hears Gretchen's voice within, singing a cruel song of a murdered child whose bones were transformed into a bird that now will fly away. For her mind, distraught like Ophelia's, the fairy-tale motif is a mirror of her own fate: the dead child, the wish to flee. At first she takes Faust for her executioner. Before dying, she wishes to nurse the infant which she had drowned, or allowed to drown, in the course of her desperate wanderings. Not until Faust calls her by name does she recognize him. But her brief joy—her words "I am saved" will be echoed later—cannot last. Thinking symbolically, she complains that his lips are cold: the chill of guilt. Characteristically, she is completely honest: "And do you know, my friend, whom you set free?" She now knows that she has drowned her child, taking full blame for it and for the death of her mother. But when she feels Faust's moist hand, another hallucination comes: "Blood is on it!" A vision of the graves of the family with hers "a little apart" is followed by one of the drowning baby and finally by a horrifying hallucination of her mother.

When Faust, torn by guilt and by fear of the returning day, tries to carry her away by force, she instinctively resists. She wishes to die, but still fears, like Egmont, the ax of the executioner. When Mephisto appears, warning that they must flee at once, her resolution is confirmed; she casts herself on God's mercy. Again Faust flees, but this time only after a direct threat from Mephisto. The Devil's "She is judged!" is refuted by a voice from above: "Is saved!" Apparently, as the "Prologue" implied, Heaven intervenes only when an individual's life is nearing an end. In any event, a supernatural voice is heard almost at the end of Part I, as near the beginning, providing a cosmic frame. Against the frequent objection that the explicit guarantee of salvation weakens the tragic force of the play, or is unnecessary, it has been urged that the spectator familiar with the original legend of Faust might take Mephisto's words as the final judgment. The last words of the scene are Gretchen's, in a voice "from within, dying away," calling the name of her lover. Clearly, they are not uttered in the tone of rejection. As for Faust, he seems to have been genuinely shaken at last. His final speeches have something of the direct simplicity of hers. Perhaps his urges will be somewhat less "dark" henceforth; perhaps he is more "aware" of the right way. But certainly the reader, as he turns to the Second Part, will be justified in regarding him with a skeptical, if not necessarily a cold eye.

7. FAUST II: THE GREAT WORLD

Faust II, GOETHE REMARKED TO ECKERMANN, PRESENTS the reader with "a loftier, broader, brighter world" than does the First Part. Only persons with a certain experience of life would know what to make of it. Over against this, as he stressed in a late letter, the Second Part is less fragmentary, more rational in its structure. One may add that the reader who knows *Faust I* really well will be best prepared to enjoy *Faust II* fully—to sense the parallelisms, reminiscences, and flashes of parody.

In another conversation with Eckermann, Goethe maintained that he was himself unable to state the basic theme of *Faust*. The thought that a man who kept striving upward could be saved was a useful one, he said, but not an "idea" permeating and motivating every single scene. The Germans are funny people, he noted wryly, always making life difficult with their deep thoughts. If only they had the courage to abandon themselves to their impressions, as he himself did as a writer! For it was not his normal poetic practice to try to incorporate some abstract principle. Then he went on to make his famous pronouncement already quoted, that the more "incommensurable" a work of poetry is, the better.

All this is delightful, and a sound warning to critics of a certain sort, but it is hardly his total judgment. Goethe was no Dadaist. At any rate, the critic must try to approximate a grasp of the intention or intentions of the work. Here two statements of Goethe's provide some help. One is contained in his famous letter to Wilhelm von Humboldt, written in 1832, only five days before his death: "these very serious jests." The other has been relatively neglected: he told Eckermann that the music for *Faust*—a great deal is called for—should be written in the style of *Don Giovanni*. "Mozart ought to have set *Faust* to music." In other words, a synthesis of tragedy and comedy, intellectual brilliance and emotion, irony and lyricism, was intended.

A further intimation of his poetic aim is included in a brief sketch written at the turn of the century. In the still unwritten Second Part, Faust was to be more aware of himself and his own motives (closer to what the "Prologue" calls clarity), was to direct his energies outward, to find exhilaration in action, and he was to experience beauty. Much later, Goethe wrote that while Faust would still be involved in "many splendid errors, actual and fantastic," he would conduct himself in a "nobler, worthier, and loftier way."

In his new sphere Faust does appear more mature, more sophisticated in the better sense. He could not renounce activism without abandoning his very self, but his

FAUST II: THE GREAT WORLD

driving force is generally more channeled and directed. To some extent, one senses, his moral education has progressed. But the "old Adam" is still very much alive, as we see near the beginning of *Faust II,* when he makes his rash lunge at the image of Helen; and more painfully near the end, when he is involved in a second crime. In this incident, the ruthless titanism of the younger Faust reasserts itself. In harmony with the cooler and more serene tone of the Second Part, Mephisto sinks from witty devil to fool and dupe, and the pact recedes very much into the background.

On another level, it has been urged by some critics that Faust has become so much a symbol of Western or universal man that he has lost his individuality. This is at best a half truth, I believe. Even when he plays the role of modern man vis-à-vis Helen's ideal Greek, his personality is still marked; and the Faust who ventures into the realm of "desolation and loneliness" to consult "the Mothers" has not lost his verve and daring.

To turn back to the text: the Second Part opens with the scene "Pleasant Landscape." Faust is discovered lying restlessly in an Alpine meadow; various nature spirits, directed by Ariel,* undertake the task of healing him and "returning him to holy light." They are successful: under their ministrations Faust recovers and is determined "To seek the highest life, for which I strive."

Of the many interpreters of this crucial scene, Santayana is the most brilliant and one of the most sympa-

---
* Shakespeare's sprite; Goethe made no attempt to conceal his many debts to Shakespeare, which are especially noticeable in *Faust.*

thetic. As he notes, the spirits, neither good nor evil in orthodox terms, heal Faust Spinozistically, as it were: pity and remorse are pointless; they are unconcerned with punishment. He must sleep, forget, and begin a new existence. It is not that Goethe thought that Faust's remorse was negligible. On the contrary, he held that the horrors of Gretchen's lot had shaken Faust to the depths, "completely paralyzed" him, so that his hero, "annihilated," had to be born again after a moral and psychological collapse. He was not submitting Faust's case to human judges, he wrote Eckermann: "Everything is compassion and the most profound pity"—perhaps a crypto-Christian point of view. If it is objected that Faust gets off pretty lightly—as in a sense he does—the counter-question runs: what else can a man do, after committing a dreadful offense, but pull himself together and start again? In this case, restitution is impossible; no higher power has punished him, and Goethe was the last to believe that a man should punish himself.

Another passage in "Pleasant Landscape" does indicate that Faust has changed, however belatedly. During the scene, dawn approaches "like thunder"—recalling the music of the spheres in the Prologue—and the sun rises in overpowering brilliance. Awakening, Faust sees "an excess of flame"; he must turn away dazzled, as he did when the Earth Spirit appeared in the fire. Now, however, he is not driven to despair; he accepts the necessity of a "veil," as Goethe had in his poem "Dedication."* In a speech in *terza rima*—which has appropriately replaced

---

* See above, p. 64.

FAUST II: THE GREAT WORLD

the less disciplined meters of the First Part—he accepts man's situation: turning away from the sun (the absolute, as it were) he can still perceive its colored reflection in the waterfall. (Similarly, in *Pandora*, Prometheus tells his followers to beware of the arrows of the sun; they are destined to see "things illuminated, not the light.") Man cannot grasp ultimate truth directly, as Faust in his titanism had once hoped, but can attain it through symbols adequate to his nature.

Reinvigorated, Faust enters the "great world" at the court of the Emperor. It was an old motif of the legend to show him as a magician or charlatan at court; again Goethe has "earned what he inherited," integrating this part of the tradition with another, in which Faust conjured up the shades of Helen and Paris, and inserting a long allegorical masque. His Emperor is weak, self-indulgent, and "has all possible qualities for losing his throne," as the poet put it. As in *Götz*, we are presented with the Holy Roman Empire at the time of the collapse of the medieval order; it is thoroughly decadent.

To ingratiate themselves at court the two adventurers follow a clever plan of action, no doubt devised by Mephisto. First he insinuates himself as court-fool, the previous jester being neatly pushed aside. Then, shrewdly exploiting the financial crisis of the Empire, he introduces Faust as a wise man and magician, a sort of braintruster, who will put things right. Their scheme is to issue vast amounts of paper money, based on still undiscovered buried treasures; and the Emperor is lackadaisical or desperate enough to let the unlikely pair try it out, though his courtiers at once distrust them.

Before the introduction of the Helen theme comes the spectacular "Masquerade." Based on Italian Renaissance carnivals, the scene displays a variety of costume, color, and metrical form. It is extremely long (over 900 lines) for its purely dramatic function of raising Faust in the Emperor's favor, and contains some rather sterile tracts of verse. Faust and Mephisto assume appropriate roles: the former as Plutus (for he claims to be the bringer of wealth); the latter as the mocker Zoilo-Thersites. As the representative of all society, the Emperor appears as Pan.

While one must admit that many of the figures who take part in the carnival are less than fascinating—the groups of gardeners, Pulcinelli, parasites, etc., and the many allegories, like the Graces, Fates, and various virtues—there is one shining exception, the Boy Charioteer, who serves Faust as his driver. "I am lavishness, I am poetry," he declares, and he scatters gifts and magic flames among the spectators—many of whom, unworthy, are unable to hold them. That the poet is seen as the prodigal giver of beauty and inspiration brings a new note into this frivolous and self-centered society. Much to Eckermann's confusion, Goethe confided to him that the Boy Charioteer "was" Euphorion, Faust's son. Of course the poet was speaking typologically, non-temporally, for Euphorion is not even born until much later in the poem. In view of this statement, however, it appears that the attractive Charioteer must "mirror" one side of Faust—a poetic and selfless potentiality of his nature which has not yet been realized.

At the climax of the action, the Emperor, as "Great Pan," is burned, or seems to be, by the flames of a foun-

FAUST II: THE GREAT WORLD

tain of magic fire, but a spell spoken by Plutus-Faust extinguishes them before he has suffered any harm. Now he thinks himself deeply in the sorcerer's debt. Some have interpreted this conflagration as an allegory of coming financial disaster or even of the French Revolution, but it is more useful to deal with the basic symbols of the scene, fire and gold. As has recently been shown, fire often carries the connotation, among others, of dangerous forces within and below society; gold is frequently associated with a dangerous but basically positive element.

In the ensuing scene, the Emperor quickly forgives Faust for the momentary fright he suffered. An aesthete in the pejorative sense, he enjoyed the thrill of seeming to be "prince of a thousand salamanders." To his utter surprise, the new paper money is everywhere; he had signed the original note, literally in a fit of absent-mindedness. Everyone rejoices in the new currency, particularly the jester whom Mephisto had replaced. *His* money he will invest in real estate; as in Shakespeare, the fool is the true wise man.

Up to this point, Faust in action has been no more impressive than he was in the First Part. He is still seeking new experiences; to find and enjoy them, he must first gain power at court, and he has not the slightest interest in assuaging the evils of the state. Until the last act, he does not betray any concern for matters of society or government. It is the vision of Helen which really stirs his energies—appropriately, since as a representative German intellectual, he is a "non-political man."

At last, in the scene "Dark Gallery" both Faust and the action really get under way. Since Mephisto has no access to classical antiquity—the pagans reside "in their own special hell," he says—Faust must look for Helen himself, by seeking out "the Mothers" in their realm of perfect emptiness, and obtain from them the image of Helen— not her actual self.

Based on materials in Plutarch, Goethe's myth of the Mothers has challenged interpreters of all sorts. Nothing indeed could sound "deeper" than an invocation of the Eternal Motherly. One should note that the poem treats the theme with a mixture of lightness and seriousness, as Faust does himself. At first he is frightened by the very word, then he becomes suspicious of Mephisto's attempts to frighten him and his mystifying play on words:

> No way! To the untrodden,
> Not to be trod upon! Away to the unbeseechable,
> Not to be besought!

Feeling that he is perhaps being used as a dupe, he nevertheless accepts a magic key,* and has to admit that he feels a thrill of awe at the prospect. Mephisto tells him to descend, adding, with sound mythic logic, that he might as well say "ascend"—direction plays no part in the realm of the Mothers. Faust disappears, off on his first really independent enterprise—an intellectual adventure, a search for things long past. It will prove successful.

During Faust's absence, the brief scene "Brightly

---

* Despite Jung, the key is hardly a phallic symbol here: see line 6261. Also, since the Mothers deal only in images, patterns, abstract forms, they are hardly full-blooded symbols of some romantically conceived *Ur*-womb.

FAUST II: THE GREAT WORLD

Lighted Halls" directs our gaze back to life at court. Since Mephisto has gained a reputation for extraordinary knowledge, he is surrounded by ladies demanding "beauty hints"; other figures want advice for the lovelorn. Light in every sense, the episode soon gives way to the much more significant "Knight's Hall," set in a dim, "Gothick" room, where spirits might easily appear, as Mephisto notes, of their own volition.

They have however been summoned for the séance. Before the Emperor and his assembled court, Faust, Mephisto, and their accomplice the court astrologer put on a play (or spectacle) within a play, in which the actors are the phantoms of Paris and Helen, though Faust violates all aesthetic distance and himself intervenes at the end. Armed with the "glowing key," Faust acts as the intermediary between the spectators and the world of empty forms; Mephisto is happy to function as prompter. The stage setting is a Doric temple; incense rises from the tripod Faust has brought back from the world of the Mothers. When he touches it with the key, a vaporous cloud rises; mysterious music is heard, and the handsome shape of Paris appears. The ladies praise his beauty, the court gentlemen, jealous, find fault with his manners.

Then Helen appears, evoking Mephisto's typical comment that she would not cost him any sleep; she is not his type. (Never, of course, will he understand the rapture she evokes in Faust, that "sensual, supersensual lover.") For Faust, she is a revelation. The world before this has been an empty nothing, he declares; may he die if he ever can adapt himself again to an existence without Helen. Compared to her, the beauty in the magic mirror was a mere "image in the foam." The impassioned speech ends in a characteristic "heightening": he owes her "the stirring of every energy, the essence of passion, affection, love, adoration, madness!" Clearly, it is not as a symbol of the Greek spirit that he loves and desires her—that aspect will be developed later—but as a woman of incredible beauty. Of course, the Helen before him is a mere shade, but he has forgotten that as he has forgotten so much else. His word "madness" was no mere rhetoric, and Mephisto has to warn him against acting out of character.

Again the courtiers are heard; naturally, it is now the women who find fault with the appearance of the female apparition. As the action develops, Faust, though warned twice again by Mephisto, is completely carried away. When Paris begins to carry off Helen, he grasps his symbolic key like a weapon and bursts into renewed passionate expression. Now he feels able, based (as he thinks) on reality, to do battle with spirits; the Mothers must grant his wish: "Who once has known her, dare not let her go!" He touches the phantom Paris with the key; an explosion throws him to the ground; the spirits dissolve. Like Sancho Panza picking up Quixote after a joust, Mephisto puts the unconscious Faust on his shoulders and closes the scene with an epigram.

As in his encounter with the Earth Spirit, Faust has tried impetuous, direct assault; this time he is even more drastically defeated. To try to overcome the forces of time and space by a single act of will is *hubris* indeed. This time at least, although he behaved like a madman, he was not the "timid, writhing worm" the Earth Spirit had called him.

FAUST II: THE GREAT WORLD

At the beginning of the Second Act we find ourselves back in Faust's high-arched study; nothing has been changed. The return to the past invites parody, just as the return to the academic atmosphere opens the door to renewed satire. Goethe took advantage of these opportunities: this scene and its successor, set in a medieval laboratory, form the comic apex of the entire poem. Mephisto, who has the first line in the scene as well as his usual last word, is in his best vein.

As he remarks, having placed Faust on an old-fashioned bed, a man paralyzed by Helen does not easily regain his senses. (Faust remains unconscious throughout the two university scenes.) It is the second time that we have seen him thus prostrate; on this occasion it was not a moral defeat which brought him low.

After commenting on the impedimenta of Faust's study, including the pen with which he signed the pact, Mephisto is given a cheerful welcome by a chorus of insects. Having put on Faust's old academic robe, he pulls a bell, which gives a supernaturally penetrating peal; doors fly open; the frightened Assistant appears. (This position is no longer Wagner's but has been taken by an overage graduate student; Wagner is now a professor in his own right; and the sub-freshman whom Mephisto had tried long ago to seduce now has his A.B. The academic machine has ground relentlessly on.) Startled, the miserable Assistant thinks a giant is standing before him; Mephisto, in reply, tries to stir up a bit of trouble by maliciously exaggerating the achievements of Wagner—"the first man now in all the learned world"—and praising him at Faust's expense. But the new men are still loyal to their former chief, despite his incomprehensible disappearance. Devoted to his "great work" of research, Wagner has been incommunicado for months.

Just when Mephisto seems ready to force his way into the laboratory, his old victim, the A.B., comes storming in. Again, as when faced with Martha Schwerdtlein, the devil is put on the defensive, for the Baccalaureus seems invincibly arrogant and egotistic: the frequency of "I" and "mine" in his conversation is frightening. After giving Professor Mephisto, as he thinks him, a rude and thorough dressing-down, the A.B. launches into an exposition of his own "philosophy":

> The world was not, till I created it;
> I led the sun up from the ocean's bed. . . .

And so on. The A.B. has escaped from Mephisto only to fall into the hands of a caricatured Fichtean idealism. (It is no coincidence that he thinks that everyone over thirty should be liquidated: Goethe sensed the relation between philosophical egotism and practical ruthlessness long before Santayana did.) Like so many others in the poem, he mirrors one aspect of Faust: his line—"Brightness before me, and the dark behind"—recalls Faust's great passage about flying.* The episode is Goethe's reckoning with the most dangerous tendency of the new generation. Characteristically, he is conciliatory even here: Mephisto, out of character, notes that even though the fermenting juice behaves absurdly, a mature wine will finally emerge.

* See above, p. 154.

FAUST II: THE GREAT WORLD

The scene shifts to the adjacent laboratory, filled with clumsy and fantastic equipment. Poor Wagner has been frightened by the bell just as his experiment seems at last about to suceed. Pathetic though he is, there is something admirable about his devotion. When Mephisto bursts in, Wagner explains anxiously but courteously that he must be very careful: "a man is being made." That means just one thing to the devil, but the professor explains that human reproduction will now take place in a more dignified, "higher" manner. He is a prude as well as a pedant. Although he describes his method in "dusty," alchemical terms, the experiment succeeds, a light begins to shine in the glass vial he is holding, and the "pretty manikin" Homunculus appears in it.

Again Goethe has put traditional materials to his own use. "Homunculi" or "bottle imps" appear frequently in alchemistic works; but Goethe's little man is entirely different. While he calls Wagner, ironically, "little father," and seems to owe his mischievous wit to his "cousin" Mephisto, he is basically a miniature Faust in his driving activity: "Since I exist, I must keep pressing on." At the same time, he is a mirror-image of Faust, for his goal is the reverse: conscious of his artificial origin, he must somehow find nature and be "really" born, while Faust at the end sheds his physical elements; only his immortal entelechy survives. Basically, Homunculus is sheer intellect, but precisely because he is that, he is conscious of his own limitation and is determined to overcome it. Only when he enters the realm of biological life, will he truly exist.

Strictly speaking, the "little fellow" should have no

personality. His precocity need not surprise us: "homunculi" were supposed to be omniscient, and beyond that, pure intellect can conceive of anything. Fortunately, Homunculus *has* a character: he is amusing, active of course, and very charming. His conversation subtly changes the comic character of the episode: wit has largely replaced satire. That he, the little Faust of the natural world, is endowed with a considerable knowledge of classical mythology, reminds us that Goethe was convinced of an intrinsic affinity linking nature and the Greeks. Homunculus is "single and double," a symbol and a person. (Usually his part is spoken by an actress concealed behind some piece of stage scenery.)

His first action is to "read the dream" of the sleeping Faust, which consists of an erotic vision of the begetting of Helen. Despite his asexual origin, the manikin is stirred by what he sees—a nice irony. "You may drive out nature by main force, but it will always return." That the vision, later repeated, is focused on Helen's procreation stresses the poem's concern with organic growth.

Homunculus fears that it would be fatal for Faust to awake from such a dream to academic reality. But, he says, it has suddenly occurred to him that it is the "Classical Walpurgis Night"; Faust must be carried to Greece. When Mephisto demurs—he has the feeling that the Greeks weren't very respectable—the imp wins him over by hinting at amorous adventures with Thessalian witches. He calls for the magic cloak; he himself will light the way like a meteor. (Obviously, he has replaced Mephisto as the manager of the action.)

As for poor Wagner, he must remain in the study. He

FAUST II: THE GREAT WORLD

has served his purpose, but is now pushed aside once for all. Up to a point, one infers, learning is invaluable, but it is inadequate as a path to beauty or life; Faust was right about that, at all events. Stuart Atkins has well noted the "supreme irony" that Wagner has not the slightest suspicion of who the unconscious man in his quarters was.

The rest of Act II is made up of the scenes of the "Classical Walpurgis Night," a series far longer than its counterpart in Part I and longer even than the Masquerade. At first one is in danger of being overwhelmed by the sheer number of characters or distracted by enigmatic references. To keep one's bearings, one must follow the three main strands of action: Faust's quest for Helen, Homunculus' for full-blooded life, and, as comic relief, Mephisto's search for erotic adventures.* A few leitmotifs also have a unifying function: the beautifully integrated form or *Gestalt*, pointing toward Helen; the swans, which already figured in Faust's dream of Leda; water as a symbol of metamorphosis; and the moon, which shines throughout. Although the figures range from gold-gathering ants and dryads to philosophers, neither the Olympian gods nor the great Greek heroes appear. Perhaps Goethe felt that including them would have decreased the stature of Faust and the significance of Helen,

---

* In this discussion I have not included various incidents, like the songs to the "Cabiri" and the argument between Neptunists and Vulcanists, not because they are unimportant but simply for lack of space. The curious reader should consult the commentaries by Atkins or Gillies and the edition of Calvin Thomas or that of Heffner, Rehder, and Twaddell.

who in a sense dominates the "Classical Walpurgis Night"; though she does not appear, she is its goal. Let it be said once for all that this cluster of fantastic scenes is not only too long in itself for most readers but contains sections which do not reach the general level of the poem. Yet there are magnificent passages: Faust's encounter with Manto, Chiron's words about Hercules, and above all the climactic ending.

Clearly, the second Walpurgis Night is even less "realistic" than the first. The ordinary functionings of time are suspended. If one says that these episodes have a dreamlike aspect, one must add that, though some individual episodes are fantastic, they are not arranged in the disjointed, illogical, Kafkaesque manner of a dream; they are ordered, and rise to a climax. And like Homunculus, Faust is moving toward realization, not trying to escape reality as he did in the earlier witches' carnival.

In talking to Eckermann, Goethe noted that the first Walpurgis Night was aristocratic, since the Devil is universally respected in it; the second is "republican," one figure being as good as another. We note also that sheer obscenity and guilt play no part in the latter fantasy; that very few of its hundreds of figures could be called evil. If the first is a sort of hell, the latter is at worst a limbo. Of course it lacks the tension and tragic force of its predecessor; its values are very different ones.

At the beginning of the "Classical Walpurgis Night," the enchantress Erichtho appears against the dark background of the Pharsalian Fields. It is the anniversary of Pompey's defeat by Julius Caesar, a battle which ended

FAUST II: THE GREAT WORLD

the last faint hopes of Roman freedom. Speaking in the six-beat iambic lines of Greek trimeter—a verse form which seems "distant" to modern ears—Erichtho assumes a gloomy tone: she depicts man's history as pointless and depressing. Suddenly countless campfires are lit; the moon rises; and a meteor appears overhead. Sensing the approach of living beings, the enchantress disappears; we hear Homunculus and Mephisto conversing above us, still airborne. (Rhymed verses replace the trimeters.) When they reach the ground, Faust suddenly revives; his first words are: "Where is she?" At Mephisto's suggestion, the three go their separate ways. Like Goethe in Italy, Faust rejoices in touching classical soil. He compares himself to Antaeus, and with an image reminding us that he is a questing hero, sets out to explore the "labyrinth" of the surrounding bonfires.

Mephisto takes over; his first words, combining prudery and lewdness, express his shock at the nakedness of the Greek figures he encounters. After he has exchanged remarks and insults with Griffins, Sphinxes, Sirens, and other unfamiliar creatures, Faust appears, euphoric: even the repulsive figures of classical myth he finds great, and "solid": "Great are the forms, and great the memories."

At the advice of the Sphinxes, Faust sets out to find Chiron, the noblest of the centaurs, and ask his help in his search. First, though, the erotic theme is reasserted. On the banks of the Peneios, nymphs take up the note of the lure of water already sounded by the Sirens. This leads to a second vision of the begetting of Helen; Faust is not sure if what he sees is a dream or a memory, but his words "the forms incomparable" indicate that this is no mere delusion—*Gestalt* signifying in Goethe a real and "solid" entity. As often in *Faust II*, the poetry has the amazing boldness of Goethe's old age; thus the swan approaching Leda moves—"Wave himself, on wavelets swaying."

The resounding earth announces the approach of Chiron, one of the most happily realized of the poem's minor figures. This man-horse is humorous, friendly, quietly ironic in his response to Faust's flattery. Now relatively sophisticated, the quester does not raise the question of Helen at once; rather, he asks to know who was the greatest of the "heroic figures" the centaur had known. In his reply, which ends with a eulogy of Hercules,[*] Chiron shows himself a poet. Faust can now ask about the fairest of women, well knowing what the answer will be. When Chiron answers, describing Helen very tangibly and saying that he has carried her on his back, she becomes "realer" to Faust and to us. Finding Faust a bit mad in his determination to win the heroine at any cost, Chiron escorts him to the prophetess Manto, thinking that she will "cure" him. Faust indignantly rejects psychotherapy; and indeed, he has been underrated. Manto regards him as a demigod, declares her love of the man "who desires the impossible," and offers to conduct him to Persephone, the goddess who might release the *real* Helen, not the shade who was subject to the Mothers. Let him use his chance better than Orpheus did! Her line—"I wait; time circles around me"—somehow lifts one

[*] Interpreted by Thomas Mann as a veiled tribute to Schiller.

FAUST II: THE GREAT WORLD

above the ordinary dimensions. The reader may be reminded of the role of time in *The Magic Mountain*.

There follows a cluster of episodes mainly important in that they form a bridge to later events. We are reminded that Mephisto is out of place in Greece; that Homunculus wants to be born, that Goethe prefers gradual evolution ("water") to geological or political revolution ("earthquake" and "fire"). In his late years, Goethe could occasionally be as heavily repetitious as Richard Wagner. Mephisto, defeated in his amorous efforts, at least finds elective affinities in the Phorkyads, the ugliest creations of Greek mythology. By adapting himself to their appearance, he has finally become "a Greek, in his own way"; he will thus be able to participate in the "Helen tragedy" which comprises Act III.

In sharp contrast to its predecessor, the scene "Rocky Coves of the Aegean Sea" is one of the splendors of the entire poem. Combining magnificent imagery with brilliant spectacle, it emphatically states the major themes of striving and rebirth. Again, there is free use of music—in the choruses—and Goethe seems also to have borrowed from painting, especially Raphael's "Triumph of Galatea," for his last scene. As Atkins has shown, "Rocky Coves" is largely in the tradition of the Renaissance "triumph." Throughout, the radiance of Goethe's favorite orb, the moon, suffuses the stage. As if to emphasize that this is a summit of the play, it remains at its zenith. Closely linked to the moon and even more important is the sea or water generally. Here it is no longer the element which lures man to death but has its opposite aspect: life and rebirth. Homunculus' climactic "wedding" with the sea is parallel to Faust's final ascension; if the latter is the Christian focus of the Second Part, the "triumph," as Beutler noted, is its pagan one.

A chorus to the moon, sung by Sirens, Nereids, and Tritons, establishes the tone. (Various other sea-creatures and nymphs appear later, as does even a cheerful group of shipwrecked sailors.) On the shore flashes the light of Homunculus, who is substituting for Faust, as it were, in this part of the action. Thales, the philosopher of gradual change, is escorting him to Nereus, hoping for advice from that crotchety old man of the sea. He however refers them to Proteus, a far more appropriate authority on matters of metamorphosis.

After the brief episode of the Cabiri,* Proteus is indeed found. True to his name, he indulges in all sorts of transformations; but unlike Mephisto's changes in Faust's study, his tricks are harmless. "Curious as a fish," he is quickly attracted by Homunculus' light. For all his teasing, Proteus is delighted by the little man and will help him. All are in excellent humor; the air is soft, pervaded by the odor of damp green vegetation—an auspiciously fertile atmosphere. The three move off together: philosopher, sea god, and bottle-imp, in what Homunculus nicely calls a "Thrice noteworthy spirit-stride."

Now the chorus sings in honor of the sun; Proteus replies by praising water, the element which eternally nourishes life. Changing himself into a dolphin, he will

---

* While these enigmatic little gods are linked with the idea of metamorphosis, the section devoted to them seems mainly satiric, as the very prosaic character of the verse devoted to them indicates.

FAUST II: THE GREAT WORLD

carry Homunculus on his back to his marriage with the sea. Thales approves:

> There, by eternal canons wending,
> Through thousand, myriad forms ascending,
> You shall attain, in time, to Man.

In these extraordinary lines, a vista is opened on the slow upward development of organic life, and the aspect of science* is established as one of the important interests of the poem. The "jests" of Homunculus and his newly found friends have suddenly become "very serious." Throughout, Goethe's "style of old age" is at its best: concentrated, sublimated, witty. When Proteus tells the manikin—"Komm geistig mit in feuchte Weite! (In spirit seek the watery distance!)—he reminds us in one word (*geistig*) that Homunculus is sheer intellect, that he is more a spirit than a physical being, and that the whole episode is symbolic.

A ring around the moon announces the approach of Galatea and her attendant nymphs. (Her father Nereus observes that some passer-by might think it merely a natural phenomenon, but "we spirits" know better: the birds of Aphrodite are accompanying his daughter.) Besides taking the part of the goddess of love—she has borrowed Aphrodite's chariot, a shell which skims over the waves—Galatea's role also anticipates Helen's. It soon appears that she inspires Homunculus to a devotion even more absolute than Faust's.

* Already introduced in debates between Thales and Anaxagoras not discussed here.

As the scene moves toward its climax, it nears the form of the cantata, with five choruses taking part; at the same time, the element of spectacle is constantly heightened. (Unfortunately, because of technical difficulties, it is hardly ever staged.) Singing of their love for the sailors they have rescued, a group of nymphs continues the erotic strain. As a sort of counterpoint, the note of renunciation is briefly heard: they must soon give up their mortal lovers, just as Nereus must resign himself to seeing his beloved daughter only at these annual festivals. In his ecstatic praise of water as the element of fertility, Thales reasserts the major theme; Homunculus stresses the beauty of the sea, Proteus its "vital moisture," the nourisher of life. Clearly, the action is moving toward the celebration of the forces of life and procreation in a "holy marriage," a *hieros gamos*.

"As if pulsing with love," Homunculus' light is now flaring up, then glowing, around Galatea's chariot. He dashes himself against it, pouring fire over the waves. In his sexual climax, he enacts a Goethean *Liebestod* (See page 117f.), dying to be reborn. Thus at the height of the triumph, all the figures are illuminated, phosphorescent. The Sirens hail Eros, "who began all things." Finally, the various choruses combine to praise the elements:

> Hail, you airs that softly flow!
> Hail, secret caves of earth below!
> Honored now and evermore
> Be the elemental four!

All are seen as irradiated by love. The chain of metamorphosis running through creation is closely linked to

FAUST II: THE GREAT WORLD

the Faustian drive in man. As the Faust of the natural world, Homunculus has played his part well. His success inclines one to be more sanguine about the outcome of Faust's search.

The Third Act combines the classical tragedy of Helen's return to Greece, employing a chorus and Greek metrical schemes, with the romantic opera of her Arcadian idyll with Faust, the birth of Euphorion, and his death after the "moment" is over. If one has the impression at first that the act could almost stand alone, one soon becomes aware of parallels, repeated motifs, and other devices linking "the Helen," as Goethe often called it, to what precedes and follows it. Actually, the drama has long been moving toward Helen's climactic appearance. Moreover, a grand parallel exists between Homunculus' finally successful efforts to "be born" and Helen's gradual development from the mere shade of Act I to a person both real and symbolic. The swan motif of Faust's repeated vision figures again in the songs of the chorus; and Mephisto's mutation—one can hardly call it a metamorphosis—to a Greek hag is an obvious bridge. As will appear, other links connect Act III to its successor.

In its sudden shift from ancient to modern times, the act is "one and double," like so many other of Goethe's works. Trite though it is, the statement that "Helen" mirrors the synthesis of Greek and Northern elements is true. Perhaps more interesting is its intention of reconciling the classic and the romantic, a far cry from Goethe's view, in his hyper-classical days, that romanticism is "sick" by definition. Finally, the freedom of Act III, with its amazing changes of scene—its ranging over 3,000 years of time—from the ordinary bonds of the theater is as striking in its way as that of the Classical Walpurgis Night. Despite or because of these dramatic liberties, it can be very effective.

At the beginning of the act, Helen comes on the stage* with a chorus of captive Trojan women; the scene is set in Sparta; the palace of Menelaus is in the background. She speaks a prologue, more or less in the manner of Euripides, to inform the audience of her immediate situation. Set in iambic trimeter and deliberately "un-German" in its diction, word order, and employment of classical rhetorical devices, her speech establishes a tone of strangeness, of *Verfremdung*, which heightens the effect produced by her abrupt, half-explained appearance:

> I, much admired and much reviled,—I, Helena,
> Come from the strand where we have disembarked but now,
> Still giddy from the restless rocking of the waves
> Of ocean.

Her husband Menelaus is still at the nearby harbor; she is here to execute his commands. After a brief lyrical interruption by the chorus, she confesses that she does not know whether she has returned as his consort and queen, or as a victim to be slain for her guilt. No sacrificial animal is at hand.

Perhaps the greatest significance of the speech is its revelation of Helen's state of mind. The "giddiness" she

---

* Goethe finally abandoned a long-planned scene in which Faust was to descend, like Orpheus, to Hades and persuade Persephone to release Helen.

FAUST II: THE GREAT WORLD

feels is by no means merely physical; she is confused about her past, her nature; even, as it later appears, about her very identity. So much has happened since her abduction by Paris, and so much more has been told of her, as her legend "growing, spun itself into a tale," that she feels a confusion which almost overwhelms her. When we first see Helen, she is not the mere shade conjured up by Faust, but a woman so obsessed with the role she has played that she almost loses her individuality. While she is also the incarnation of classic beauty, she is no mere allegory: to Goethe the symbol not only "means" but "is." Like certain characters in Mann's *Joseph*, Helen thinks mythically; at the beginning of the act she is not sure who she really is, but she develops into an authentic person.

Apprehensively but with dignity and courage, Helen enters the palace. After the chorus has sung, ironically in the circumstances, of the joys of home-coming, she returns, deeply shocked: she has encountered horror, "rising from the womb of old Night." In time she is able to tell what has happened. In the gloomy, silent palace she encountered a veiled woman of imposing stature and ugliness, who drove her away from her marriage couch. It is Mephisto, disguised as Phorkyas, playing the part of the housekeeper of the palace. At once Phorkyas-Mephisto devotes himself to frightening and bewildering Helen. (While his most obvious motive is to weaken Helen so much that she will turn to Faust for protection, there are others: the instinctive hostility between ugliness and beauty, and the antagonism of this Northern devil toward the ideal which Helen embodies.) Reviling the chorus as cheap, damaged goods, as lustful wenches, he indirectly insults Helen; sarcastically praising the wisdom and discretion of her past, he excites painful memories. Recalling her wanderings, Helen feels that her will to live is weakening, her identity doubtful:

> Was I all that? and am I now? and shall I henceforth be
> The dream and terror of those town-destroying men?

With deliberate sadism, Phorkyas-Mephisto recounts the contradictory tales of her loves and adventures, reserving the most confusing and irrational to the end: that she had lived, in double form, in Troy and Egypt at once; that Achilles, though a shade, had loved her "against every decision of fate." This last myth affords a precedent for Faust; but the psychological torture has become too much. That union had been formed by phantoms, Helen says: she feels herself becoming a phantom even in her own eyes. Like Gretchen when she too was tormented by an evil spirit, she faints.

Too heroic to remain long in psychological disarray, and hailed by the chorus as the "shape of all shapes" which the sun ever shone upon, Helen soon recovers. Phorkyas-Mephisto mixes flattery and threats of Menelaus' revenge adroitly: Helen will die a noble death, but the others will be strung up on the rafters, to die like snared birds. Ignobly the women of the chorus, who have just exchanged the most robust of insults with Phorkyas-Mephisto, flatter him; Helen retains her stature. Their only hope is to place themselves under the protection of the ruler of a host of Northern conquerors: the mas-

FAUST II: THE GREAT WORLD

querading devil eloquently praises him, the blond handsomeness of his followers, and the Gothic architecture of his castle. (At one stroke we have been projected into the Middle Ages.) A blaring of trumpets falsely convinces the chorus that Menelaus is approaching; Helen at last consents to the scheme. In one of the many striking transformations which mark the act, clouds cover the stage. The chorus, in its last lyric of the scene, evokes the motif of the swan. Bewildered by the clouds, it is frightened, when they lift, to find itself shut in by dark, sheer ramparts. (Space can be manipulated as easily as time; they are now within Faust's castle.) With the ominous repetition of the word "imprisoned," the first section comes to an end.

Actually, danger exists only in their own little minds; the "Inner Courtyard" surrounding them will be the scene of Helen's triumph. She seems unimpressed by the "rich, fantastic" medieval structures surrounding them, though she does speak to Mephisto-Phorkyas with a certain respect, now that he has actually carried out his promise. Essentially, however, her mood is that of weariness: "I wish the wandering's end, I wish for rest alone."

Instead of finding rest, she is immediately confronted with the irruption of medieval pageantry, carefully staged by Mephisto. Handsome pages appear, at once diverting the lightheaded ladies of the chorus from their fears; they are stirred both by the youths' beauty and the richness of the throne they carry in; its draperies "over-overflow," as their lyric strikingly puts it. Helen mounts the throne.

When Faust appears in his medieval costume, the leader

of the chorus declares that he will always reach his goal, in love as in war. (As in his encounter with Manto, his new impressiveness is stressed.) His opening speech, in blank verse, reasserts the modern note; these are the first lines in the act not set in classical meters. With him is the watchman Lynceus, in chains: dazzled by Helen's beauty, he has neglected to announce her arrival. With an extravagance which reflects (and perhaps parodies) a medieval knight's subservience to his lady, Faust lays his servant's life in Helen's hands.

Speaking in rhymed strophes, somewhat in the mood of a troubadour, Lynceus equates Helen with the sun, with a goddess. She pardons him, moved not by these conceits but by her sense that he is yet another victim of her fatal though god-given beauty. Immediately Faust declares himself her vassal.

After a second speech by Lynceus, Faust takes his place by Helen's side. In answer to her request that he explain why Lynceus' words sounded so strange, with one word "caressing" another—the erotic image is important—he teaches her how to rhyme:

> FAUST: Our spirits look not forward, not behind,
>   And only in the present—
> HELEN: Joy we find.

Obviously, the rhymes mirror Faust's successful wooing, as well as the reconciliation of ancient and modern. The chorus sings of their union; they scorn to conceal their "secret joys." (The speed of the action reminds us that we are in a world of magic.) From Faust's phrase "only in

FAUST II: THE GREAT WORLD

the present," we must infer that his restlessness has been overcome, the pact forgotten. This impression is strengthened when he adds that it is one's duty to exist, even if such real being (*Dasein*) should last but a moment. Even if he does not quite ask that the moment be prolonged, he implies a hope that it may, and of course that it is "wonderful." Strictly speaking, the wager is lost; but Mephisto's writ does not run in Greece, and he has become Faust's servant rather than his antagonist.

At any rate, the word "moment" brings Mephisto-Phorkyas on the stage, not to claim Faust's soul but to warn him that Menelaus' army is approaching. It is an empty threat: the "army" is a phantom, and Faust knows it. In response he calls his own soldiers together and assigns various parts of Greece as fiefs to the several Germanic tribes, all subject to Helen's rule. He exploits the chance of impressing her with their martial might:

> The light upon their armor breaking,
> They plundered realm on realm, at will:
> They come, and lo! the earth is quaking. . . .

If this unexpected pride in German military prowess is distasteful, one should recall that it is part of Faust's wooing, not a political program.

After another ode sung by the chorus we hear Faust's great poem, an evocation of Greece, of the golden age, of a fulfilled existence. One of the glories of the whole drama, it pictures the landscape, mountains and forests, nymphs and animals. In strongly accented five-beat lines, rich in imagery, it is both vigorous and idyllic; this is no pale pastoral of the Rococo mode. Above all it presents human beings, happy, "whole," in harmony with themselves and with nature:

> Here joy, descending to each generation,
> Smiles from bright faces still without surcease;
> Each is immortal in his age and station,
> And they are sane and happy, and at peace.

In this "pure light," he continues, the child easily attains the strength of his father—a foreshadowing of the birth of his own son. No sharp distinction can be drawn between such men and gods; thus Apollo could associate with the shepherds as an equal. All the realms of being interact.

Taking his place at Helen's side, Faust urges that they put the past behind them. She, the child of a god, belongs only to "the first world," the golden age. The last line of his poem—"Arcadian be our bliss, our liberty!"—is also a signal: in another magical transformation, the scene shifts; the brief Arcadian idyll of Faust and Helen begins.

As one would expect, Helen's development from a figure of myth to a person real in some sense is mirrored in the language she speaks. In the first scene her speech, closely modeled on the Greek, is almost painfully abstract to the modern ear:

> The purest water from the sacred fountain be
> In lofty urns; and further, also ready hold
> The well-dried wood. . . .

FAUST II: THE GREAT WORLD

Toward the end of the episode she is rather laconic and reserved. As her diction approaches Faust's, it inevitably appears more natural to the German reader. This linguistic realization is brief, for during her appearance in the Arcadian idyll, she speaks mainly in lines designed to be sung; they have a libretto-like quality. After the death of her son, she reverts, just before returning to Hades, to Greek trimeter; but her anxieties about her identity, dissipated by her union with Faust, do not return. She leaves the stage possessed of full tragic stature.

As the Arcadian scene* opens, Phorkyas-Mephisto tells the chorus, in trimeter, how Faust and Helen have withdrawn into a subterranean underworld of grottoes, halls, and courtyards. In this magical retreat Helen has borne a son, who has already become a handsome, daring youth with a golden lyre; an aureole shines over his head, the symbol of genius and of danger. (Recalling the Boy Charioteer,** one sees in him at once the genius of poetry. He is allegorical, Goethe said, rather than human.) His precocity reminds the chorus of the infant Hermes, whose thievish exploits are the subject of another ode. When they call their tale a "charming lie," we are again reminded not to take the action too literally.

Suddenly, music is heard from the cave; the stage direction tells us that there will be a full musical accompaniment to the ensuing action. We are now in the realm of opera; apparently Goethe planned that singers should

* Often entitled "Shadowy Grove" or "Arcadia" in modern editions.
** See p. 182f.

take over the various roles in this section of the drama. Accordingly, Phorkyas-Mephisto declares that the day of the old gods has passed; the lines are now rhymed without exception, generally short, and clearly written to be sung. Faust, Helen, and Euphorion appear. Ironically, Faust, of all people, must repeatedly warn his son to be moderate; the youth is full of aspiration, an "overheightened" Faust, yearning for exploits in love and war. Pursuing a recalcitrant girl, he is momentarily enveloped in fire, like the Emperor before him. Shaking off the flames of passion, he sounds the Excelsior-note—"I will rise up ever higher"—and asserts his desire for battle, even for death. Seeing wings above him, he leaps wildly into the air; the chorus recalls the fate of Icarus; he crashes to earth at his parents' feet. His body disappears; the aureole rises into the skies; his garment, mantle, and lyre remain on the ground; as Phorkyas-Mephisto later remarks, they will evoke imitation, if not real talent.

Up to this point, Euphorion has represented romantic poetry, with its exaggerated Faustianism and desire for the infinite. It is the poetry of romantic Hellenism, recalling Hölderlin and much of Keats and Shelley. Now the poem identifies him specifically with Byron. Euphorion's last words, "from the depths," implore his mother not to leave him alone; the answering dirge begins by echoing the words "not alone" and recalls the genius and courage but also the tragic flaws of Lord Byron, who had recently perished in the struggle for Greek independence. But the last lines of the chorus assert the immortality of poetry. Life and creativity are reaffirmed, as they were in the funeral rites of Mignon, in *Meister's Apprentice-*

FAUST II: THE GREAT WORLD

ship. Whether *Faust* as a whole gains or loses by this shift of focus is another matter.

Now the music stops; the idyll has ended. In a few lines Helen takes leave of Faust; Euphorion will not be "alone" in Hades. Her garment and veil, symbols of the classical tradition,* remain in his hands. Completely out of his role, Mephisto-Phorkyas, momentarily a classicist, admonishes Faust never to relinquish the heritage, which will raise him above all ordinary things. Transformed into a cloud, the garment now raises him in another sense, and carries him out of our sight.

As Santayana has remarked, Goethe's wisdom was never more apparent than in his realization that the classical past cannot be revived; even in art, it can be recaptured only for "moments." And Faust would seem to have learned through intense experience that though beauty is an integral part of the fulfilled life, it is not all-sufficient.

Quickly the Arcadian world dissolves. Like Helen, the leader of the chorus will continue to exist in Hades; for as she says, fidelity as well as achievement insure that a given individual will survive. To use one of Goethe's favorite words, the true entelechy is indestructible; as he said to Eckermann: "if I am unceasingly active to my end, nature is under the obligation [!] to assign me another form of existence. . . ." But the ordinary members of the chorus, with no special moral or intellectual merit, are subject to a different law. They were never authentic personalities, for they were "real" only physically.

* For the special significance of the veil image, see above, p. 64.

To present this literal return to nature, Goethe brings the act to a close in a Bacchanal. Representing a relapse into anonymity, it is intensely Dionysiac. Employing an insistent eight-beat trochaic line, the meter used in *Faust* to express incessant movement and chaos, the four groups of the chorus celebrate their imminent reduction to the elements of earth, air, water, and fire, and associate themselves with four groups of nymphs—Dryads, Oreads, Naiads, and spirits of the vine. It is metamorphosis in reverse. Significantly, their song ends with the theme of wine, and is dominated by it. Dionysos is invoked by name; it is a true orgy:

> The cloven hoofs tread down all inhibition,
> All the senses reel and stagger. . . .

The climax equals in power the festival of Galatea at the end of Act II; here dissolution has replaced procreation. After the curtain falls, Mephisto, in the proscenium, lifts mask and veil as if to emphasize that the "classic-romantic phantasmagory" had been a mere illusion, all managed by him. But as we have seen, he has a way of being wrong about major questions.

The main function of Act IV is to serve as a bridge between the world of beauty and that of action. More concretely, it puts Faust in a position to carry out the grandiose project of land-reclamation, in Act V, with which his earthly career ends. To do this he needs land from the Emperor, and a free hand for action.

Parallel to this shift in his aspirations is Gretchen's

FAUST II: THE GREAT WORLD

return to his consciousness and the gradual fading of Helen. When the cloud which has brought him from Arcadia has gently set him down in high mountain country, it divides. Speaking still under the spell of Greece, in trimeters, Faust describes how one part assumes the shape of a woman of classical beauty—Juno, Leda, or Helen—the other a less heroic but lovely form, suggesting "beauty of the soul," linked, Faust says, to what is best in him. Gretchen is not mentioned, but her symbolic triumph is clear.

When Mephisto arrives grotesquely, on seven-league boots, classical meters are abandoned for rhymed forms. (Significantly, references to the Bible are frequent in the last two acts; the Greek myth recedes.) A geological duologue—again Vulcanism versus gradualism—seems irrelevant at first but is quickly connected to the theme of chaos against order. During his return (his last "flight" until after his death) Faust has been annoyed, indeed disgusted, by seeing the waste of the vast potential energy of the tides: he is determined to harness them with dikes and other works, to assert man's will over the sea.

Mephisto thinks this a simple task. By exploiting the troubles of the Emperor, Faust can again put him into his debt and gain a stretch of coast as his reward. For, as a burst of martial music off stage has indicated, war has broken out. The decay of the state, perhaps hastened by the introduction of Mephisto's paper money (see pp. 181–83), has led to a revolt: "Volcanic" forces are loose in the political sphere. Using all sorts of hocus-pocus, Mephisto, with Faust as an accomplice, enables the Emperor to defeat the pretender to his throne, in a battle in which images of fire and mirage are significant. While the actual ceremony is not shown, Faust does receive his coastal fief.

The Empire appears as decadent and corrupt, though Goethe's regard for Imperial traditions and usages familiar to him since boyhood is also evident. The use of rhymed Alexandrines, a form felt to be obsolete and artificial, is significant.

The last major section of the poem to be written, Act IV is the weakest element of *Faust*. It tends to tell us at length of matters either irrelevant or already known. When it focuses on Faust however, the act does maintain the general level; his lines have the vigor one has come to expect of him. While he is not demonstrably "better," he is more mature and incisive, curtly dismissing Mephisto's suggestion of further sensual pleasures. Now he desires power: action, not glory; least of all does he wish enjoyment, which makes men "ordinary." Though Mephisto has regained part of his power on Northern soil, Faust no longer has any respect for him. The poem indicates that the new scope of Faust's ambitions derives from his ennobling experience in Greece. Despite Thomas' witty remark—"nor is it clear that familiarity with the Greek spirit . . . especially disposes the mind to large works of engineering"—there is no doubt that Faust's classical education has helped to fit him for the *vita activa*. While there is nothing explicitly altruistic about his project, it shows him resolved to assert order over chaos, man over the elements.

FAUST II: THE GREAT WORLD

Act V is the climax of the entire poem. In rapidly shifting scenes, which contrast Faust's dynamic new commonwealth to the old order it displaces, and present his final moment of self-assertion, his death, and the ascension of his "immortal part," it brings his long earthly career to its end, indicating at the same time that Faust's monad will continue its dynamic activity. By restating the motifs of striving and salvation and of the wager, and picturing Gretchen's return, the poet rounds off the action; but the poem is never brought to a full stop, as a Greek tragedy is: its end makes clear that the Faustian process never ceases. Act V is profoundly dialectical, portraying Faust's renewed guilt and his moment of moral magnificence, his blindness and his insight, his stirring reassertion of "this-worldliness" and his translation to a supernatural sphere. The tensions could hardly be greater and the irony, particularly at the time of Faust's death, is tragic indeed. At the same time the act can be lighthearted in its playing with words and in the depiction of Mephisto's grotesque defeat. Its language is an amazing fusion of the old Faustian energy and the symbolic style of Goethe's later poetry.

The scene "Open Country" shows us Faust's great project as it appears to an idyllic couple, remnants of an older world. Philemon and Baucis,* whose land Faust covets, are thoroughly good, kindly people, pious and

---

* The names are used only to establish them as belonging to the type of Ovid's old couple; there is nothing classical about them. Similarly, the watchman here is called Lynceus because he has the same function as the "lynx-eyed" lookout of Act III.

conservative. Explaining the vast changes Faust has made along the shore, Philemon stresses the achievement, his wife the suffering and sinister magic involved. Her line "Human victims had to bleed" suggests the most barbarous sacrifices, but may be only her superstitious interpretation of inevitable accidents. In any case, the ambiguity is appropriate: we cannot be sure how real the new land behind Faust's dikes is. As the sun sets, they proceed to the chapel to pray to the "God of old"—a form of symbolic resistance to the new regime.

Hearing the ringing of the chapel bell, Faust is infuriated. Though now a hundred years old, he is more imperious than ever. For all his splendid estates and his palace, he cannot be at peace until he owns the property of his neighbors, set on high, "original" ground. Incorrigibly romantic, a man who demands all or nothing, he feels that his whole existence will be ruined without it. Probably it is not the scrap of land as such which he desires; rather he resents the existence of a "natural," idyllic life which he cannot share. His malaise is acute: "Would I were far away from here!" Faust's despairing speech is preceded and followed by Lynceus' naively optimistic lines praising his master's happiness. Of course Faust's covetousness is another symptom, a particularly unlovely one, of that dynamism which is his strength and his curse.

When Mephisto appears, accompanied by his ruthless servants, the "Three Mighty Fellows," another cause of Faust's uneasiness becomes clear: he is still unwillingly dependent on the uncanny magic powers involved; old

FAUST II: THE GREAT WORLD

Baucis' fears were essentially well-founded. Absorbed in his own labors, Faust has not prevented his associates from engaging in piracy as a sideline. Cleverly flattering his master and playing on his dislike of the bell, with its otherworldly, Christian burden, Mephisto elicits Faust's command to shift the old couple to another property. While he says nothing about using force, his confession that he is "growing tired of acting justly" gives *carte blanche* to his infernal helpers.

"Deep Night," the following episode, reminds us by its title that Faust's world is growing blacker in every sense. Ironically, it begins with the lovely song of Lynceus, celebrating the joys of seeing—a characteristic Goethean theme—and the beauty of the world. Suddenly Lynceus sees sparks through the "double night" of the lindens surrounding Philemon's cottage, then a "wildly burning hell" of flames; the hut, trees, and chapel are consumed. Faust admits, to himself, that his impatient act was wrong; but with almost incredible self-deception, he envisions the happiness of the old couple in their new home. At once, with brutal frankness, Mephisto destroys this illusion: the old people had resisted; in the ensuing fight, they and a guest of theirs were killed. Again, Faust has helped to destroy a peaceful, "cottage" existence; three new victims have joined Gretchen's family in death. He curses Mephisto and his accomplices and, when alone, half-admits his guilt: "Quick ordered, and too quickly done!"

On this occasion retribution comes at once; the scene "Midnight" follows without interruption. From the smoke of the burning hut four gray women, reminiscent of the witches in *Macbeth,* take shape—Want, Debt,* Distress, and Care. Only Care has the power to injure a rich man; the others slink away, but their last word is "death." Faust, who has overheard it, admits in a monologue that he is not yet truly free; still partially dependent on magic, he is not an autonomous person. Precisely because he is still linked to Mephisto he is the prey of irrational fears, and when he hears a mysterious figure at the door, he is shaken; but he is still defiant. In his line of self-admonition—"Be careful now, and speak no magic spell"—he makes his first clear break with Mephisto's world. By encountering Care—for it is she of course—simply as a man, not as a mage, he makes himself vulnerable to her; it is a decisive step toward freedom. Beginning what Faust sarcastically calls her "litany," Care describes her powers, and we know from his second monologue in the First Part that he has long had to struggle against the self-destructive *Angst* which she represents. Faust's reply is one of his strongest. Beginning with the exaggerated confession that he has only rushed recklessly through life up to the present, he defines his own belief. It is foolish for a man to turn his eyes to another world** or to imagine beings like himself "above the clouds." Let him stand firmly on this earth, which a real man can comprehend by natural means (a favorite belief of Goethe's).

* As most editors interpret the word (*Schuld*). It also means "guilt," but that element is subsumed in the role of Care. By stressing "care" (or obsessive worry; see above, p. 45f.) rather than guilt, Goethe makes his focus psychological rather than strictly ethical.

** They would be dazzled by its radiance. See "Pleasant Landscape."

FAUST II: THE GREAT WORLD

Let him live courageously and fully, never satisfied by any instant. For all his self-assertion, Faust no longer strikes the note of irresponsible titanism.

What does "magic" mean, one asks oneself, in the context of the total poem? A complete answer is impossible, but the magical would seem to embrace not only superstition but whatever seems irrational from the point of view of humanistic dignity. On the level of behavior, it would also include "cheating" of any sort, trying to live without paying for one's experiences.

Twice again Care tries to demoralize him; when he declares that he will never acknowledge her power, she counters by demonstrating it: she blinds him. In a still more magnificent response, he speaks of a bright light within him; we recall that the Lord spoke of "leading him to clarity." As Emrich infers from this passage, he is now blind to the details of restless activity, but able at last to see the whole. "Faust is free." Wounded but victorious, he is determined—at midnight!—to order his vassals to renew their labor.

In his exuberance, he has forgotten the ominous word "death." The scene "Great Courtyard before the Palace," with the stage lit only by torches and the sinister chorus of grave-digging Lemures,* is a weird setting for his approaching end. While it is deeply ironic that Faust deceives himself almost to the end, Mephisto is still more seriously mistaken. Presumably the project, built with magic aid, will soon be destroyed by the "water-devil";

* Near-skeletons, but still possessed of sinews. Their two songs go back to the gravediggers' song in *Hamlet*.

but the idea of such a struggle against the elements will endure.

When the blind Faust first appears, he mistakes the clatter of the Lemures' spades for the sound made by his workers. Still ruthless, he demands that new laborers be found: "Reward, entice, or force them here!" He expects that the great canal, which is to drain a pestilent swamp nearby, will be lengthened every day.

In his last speech, Faust rises to a vision of "standing among free people on free land," living with Faustian energy, not safely but in free activity, and with the sense of a commonly shared effort which he himself had never possessed. (Actually the vision is radically different from the authoritarian "reclamation authority" he has established.) Like Moses, he can see but may not enter the Promised Land. But if confronted with such an existence, he admits, he could well ask that the moment be prolonged. With a flash of the old *hubris* (he remains far from perfect to the end) he declares that his work will last for aeons, and concludes that in the anticipation of such happiness he now enjoys the highest moment.° He falls back; the Lemures lay him on the ground.

Naturally Mephisto thinks that he has won, but he is too much the nihilist to rejoice in his triumph. When the Lemures sing "It is past," he returns to the old theme of nothingness; time, creation, and destruction all bore him; rather a void than the senseless cycles of life.

The scene "Interment" belies its solemn title. After a second song by the Lemures, Mephisto speaks a long,

° "Anticipation" (*Vorgefühl*) and "now" seem to cancel each other out; no wonder Mephisto is misled.

FAUST II: THE GREAT WORLD

mock-serious tirade. Fearing that he will lose Faust's soul at the last moment, he protests against the slackness of the times and summons up troops of devils, fat and thin, to help him. The "gruesome jaws of Hell" open. These stage effects, borrowed from baroque spectacles, medieval moralities, and grotesque frescoes, contribute to the sense of parody. Hoping to reverse the process of metamorphosis, Mephisto orders his legions to seize Faust's soul, tear out its wings—again the butterfly image*—and reduce it to a nasty worm.

With a striking baroque effect, a radiant "glory from above" appears, opposite to the jaws of Hell. Singing in the short lines typical of the poem's choruses, angels scatter the flaming roses of love on the infernal host. After brief resistance, the lesser devils flee, pell-mell and "arse-first." Mephisto himself is overcome by lust for the boyish angels: he can pervert love but cannot entirely withstand it.

The angels, bearing Faust's "immortal element," disappear. In a last, grimly humorous monologue, Mephisto admits that his undertaking has been foolish, in fact mad. The witty devil of Part I has become a mere dupe. Evil, the scene implies, is essentially stupid and ridiculous. Some readers find it too light in tone; but the real issue was decided by Faust's defeat of Care. In "Interment" we are presented with the parodistic acting out of an already decided battle.

The final scene, "Mountain Ravines," presents Faust's ascension, borne by soaring angels; it is the ultimate

* See its use in "Holy Longing," pages 117f.

climax of the motif of flying. Moving spirally upward, we encounter various Fathers of the Church, the chorus of Blessed Boys, angels of different degrees of perfection, and Penitent Women, each at the appropriate height in this amazing vertical action. At its summit, the Mater Gloriosa appears; soon thereafter Gretchen, as one of the penitents. Scenery and language have expressionistic force, reminding one of the landscape and figures of El Greco. The first chorus expresses the vertiginous illusion that the whole landscape is in motion:

> Woods clamber tremblingly,
> Crags bear down weightily,
> Roots cling tenaciously,
> Trunks make a density. . . .

It is a challenge with which the modern stage or film can cope. The style is concentrated, bold, lapidary:

> As with its own strong urge the tree-trunk
> Climbs up the air, erect and tall,
> Just so it is, that love almighty
> Which all things forms and fosters all.

In frequently repeated leitmotifs love is established as the dominating center of the scene. Even floods and bolts of lightning are interpreted by Pater Profundus as "heralds of love," much as Michael, in the Prologue in Heaven, saw storms as the expression of the "gentle movement" of God's day.

Many have felt that the Christian tone of "Mountain Ravines" is inappropriate to *Faust,* or wondered at least that Goethe chose to close his greatest work in this way.

FAUST II: THE GREAT WORLD

To Eckermann the poet gave a technical reason, so to speak: to avoid vagueness, to gain solidity, he employed "the sharply outlined Christian-ecclesiastical figures and ideas." He showed the greatest empathy with them, one must add, even with that self-tormenting ascetic, Pater Ecstaticus. Since moreover Goethe professedly conceived of the ideal in feminine form, the Mater Gloriosa was a natural symbol for the forgiving "love from above" or grace which Faust needed. For Faust does not perfect himself; while his ceaseless striving was necessary, if he was to be saved, it would not have sufficed in itself. Grace is not a dogmatic concept here, but symbolizes what is given to man unearned, as when Wilhelm Meister found a kingdom rather than the she-asses he had sought. Rejecting a merely Enlightened interpretation of *Faust*, Goethe remarked "in old age we all become mystics."

Nevertheless, the dynamic heaven toward which Faust is rising is anything but orthodox; a glance at Dante's paradise makes that clear. In this sphere movement and action prevail. Faust does not repent or undergo conversion; rather, he experiences a series of metamorphoses after his physical death as before it. The familiar image of the chrysalis appears again. The "Eternal Womanly" at the end is a symbol of love, purer than Faust's striving love but complementary to it. For love comprises Faustian *élan* as well as the love of God; love is the mover of the universe. Thus the poem, ending, links its stress on heightening upward development with the affirmation of love. These are the two great themes of all Goethe's work.

NOTES

(Works not identified in detail are more fully described in the bibliography.)

Page
2 *early verdict:* in *The Use of Poetry and the Use of Criticism* (London, 1933), p. 99.
reversed himself: See *Goethe as the Sage,* Hamburg, [1955].
Irving Babbitt: Rousseau and Romanticism (Boston, and New York, 1924), pp. 170 f., 360 f.

3 *"near-masterpiece":* C. Fadiman in *The Nation,* CXXXIV (1932), 678.

5 *avoided . . . patterns:* E. Staiger in the "Gedenkausgabe," of Goethe, I, 740.
crypto-lyricism: See B. Fairley, *Goethe's Faust* (Oxford, 1953), pp. 7–9.
poetry raised: see E. M. Wilkinson, in *Publications of the English Goethe Society,* 1946, pp. 100–02.

8 *In England:* S. Howe, *Wilhelm Meister and his English Kinsmen,* (New York, 1930).

10 *Croce: Goethe* (New York, 1923), p. 140.

NOTES

Page
- 25 *classic virtues:* see J. Urzidil in *Germanic Review,* XXIV (1949), 184–99.
- 31 *"poetic justice":* see E. Beutler in the "Gedenkausgabe," IV, 1074 f.
- 32 *Ku-Klux Klan:* J. T. Hatfield, *PMLA,* XXVII (1922), 735–39.
- 38 *associated with Christ:* H. Schöffler, *Die Leiden des jungen Werthers* (Frankfurt a.M., 1939).
- 39 *pointed out:* Fairley, *A Study of Goethe* (Oxford, 1947), p. 16.
- 47 *Gundolf:* in his *Goethe* (Berlin, 1916), p. 185.
- 50 *shabby town:* see W. Bode, *Das Leben in Alt-Weimar* (Leipzig, 1922); W. H. Bruford, *Germany in the Eighteenth Century,* pp. 30 ff.
- 53 *close to Fielding:* see Guy Stern, "Fielding, Wieland and Goethe" (Columbia diss., 1954).
- 56 *Heinz Politzer: Germanic Review,* XXXVII (1962), 42–54.
- 58 *well observed:* by W. Rasch, *Goethes Torquato Tasso* (Stuttgart, 1954), p. 70
- 61 *essay on "Tasso": Publications of the English Goethe Society,* 1946, pp. 96–127.
- 62 *intensified . . . "Werther":* see E. M. Wilkinson, *Mod. Lang. Review,* XLIV (1949), 305–28.
- 63 *durative form:* Rasch, p. 170.
- 72 *Magnus: Goethe as a Scientist* (New York, 1949), p. 84. *Fairley:* in *A Study of Goethe,* p. 130.
- 74 *Santayana: Three Philosophical Poets,* p. 175.
- 78 *Priapus:* see Thomas Mann, *The Permanent Goethe* (New York, 1948), p. xxv.
- 82 *half-real world:* K. May in Goethe, ed. cit., VI, 1190 f.
- 95 *the very center:* H. W. Nevinson, *Goethe: Man and Poet* (London, [1931]), p. 152.

NOTES

Page

104 *Walther Killy:* see *Die Neue Rundschau,* LXXII (1961), 636–50.
106 *industrial masses:* K. May, *loc. cit.,* p. 1206 f.
107 *analogy:* ibid., p. 1209.
112 *Staiger:* Goethe, *ed. cit.,* I, 743.
119 *careful correctness:* Staiger, ibid., p. 748.
124 *Gundolf:* Goethe, p. 715 f.
well-adjusted: A. Henkel, *Entsagung* (Tübingen, 1954), p. 139.
126 *economic depression:* E. Neff, *A Revolution in European Poetry* (New York, 1940), p. 103.
127 *Viëtor:* Goethe the Poet, p. 264.
129 *"Novella":* see E. Staiger, *Meisterwerke deutscher Sprache* (Zürich, 1957), pp. 135–62.
130 *Biedermeier:* G. Müller, *Kleine Goethebiographie* (Bonn, 1955), p. 248.
134 *acute critic:* S. Atkins, *Goethe's Faust* (Cambridge, [Mass.], 1958), p. 271.
135 *Santayana: Three Philosophical Poets,* p. 188.
elucidates the first: Fairley, *Goethe's Faust, passim.*
138 *light and dark:* ibid., p. 33.
140 *Gillies:* in his *Goethe's Faust,* p. 17.
147 *renewed in revelation:* Atkins, p. 166.
in earnest: Santayana, p. 164.
151 *discontent:* B. v. Wiese, *Die deutsche Tragödie . . .* (Hamburg, 1952), 134 f.
152 *"Goethe's Major Plays":* pp. 165ff.
154 *Santayana:* p. 167.
155 *Beast images:* see Atkins, p. 61.
156 *Beutler:* in his edition of *Faust* (Wiesbaden, 1948), p. lv.

225

NOTES

Page
- 157 *Titian's or Giorgione's:* see Witkowski's edition of *Faust* (Leipzig, 1929), II, 417 f.
- 158 *Gillies:* p. 61.
- 159 *Peacock:* p. 189.
  Santayana: p. 169.
- 160 *five main actions:* see *Goethe Bicentennial Studies* (Bloomington, 1950), pp. 237–325.
- 163 *"worser self":* Atkins, p. 82.
- 165 *Gretchen, meanwhile:* see E. Trunz in the "Hamburg edition" of Goethe, III, 518 f.
- 167 *brutal:* Gillies, p. 63.
- 169 *Fairley: Goethe's Faust,* pp. 72–5.
- 170 *"Sound and imagery":* Trunz, *loc. cit.,* p. 522.
- 172 *Lilith:* Beutler in the "Gedenkausgabe," V. 765.
  distraught and clairvoyant: Trunz, *loc. cit.,* p. 530.
- 174 *realism:* F. C. Endres, *Symbolik von Goethe's Faust* (Zürich, 1940), p. 5.
- 179 *reasserts itself:* Gundolf, p. 775.
  Santayana: p. 170.
- 183 *recently been shown:* by W. Emrich, *Die Symbolik von Faust II* (Bonn, 1957), p. 185–212.
- 188 *frequency of "I":* Trunz, *loc. cit.,* p. 551.
- 190 *pure intellect:* see Gundolf, pp. 769–71.
- 191 *Atkins:* p. 152.
- 195 *Atkins:* p. 182.
- 196 *Beutler: loc. cit.,* p. 735 f.
- 201 *she develops:* see O. Seidlin's excellent article in *PMLA,* LXII (1947), 183–212.
- 204 *world of magic:* see Atkins' interpretation of much of *Faust II* as a dream-play, with important analogies to Calderón's dramas.

NOTES

Page
- 209 *Santayana:* p. 178.
- 211 *"Volcanic" forces:* Emrich, pp. 373–78.
- 212 *Thomas' . . . remark: Goethe's Faust,* II (Boston, 1897), p. xliv.
- 214 *resents the existence:* Emrich, p. 401 f.
- 217 *Emrich infers:* p. 397.
  "Faust is free": Gillies, p. 199.
- 218 *Like Moses:* See Burdach, "Faust und Moses," in the *Proceedings* of the Prussian Academy, 1912.
- 221 *not perfect himself:* Beutler, *ed. cit.,* V, 751.

A BRIEF LIST OF WORKS IN ENGLISH

1. *Goethe's Own Writings:*

There is no really adequate English translation of the collected works, but the Bohn Edition (14 vols.; London, 1848–90) may perhaps be called standard, *faute de mieux:* the "People's Edition" (1882), the *Works* (ed. H. H. Boyesen, 1885), and the so-called "Weimar Edition" (n.d.) were based mainly on it.

Bayard Taylor's *Faust*° and Carlyle's translation of the two *Wilhelm Meister* novels have many good qualities but are "Victorian." Louis MacNeice's *Faust* is one of the best but omits about a third of the poem; C. F. MacIntyre's and Philip Wayne's renderings of *Faust I* (only) are also fine. No one has successfully translated any great number of Goethe's lyrics, but dozens of poets, from

---

° Unfortunately, Stuart Atkins' revision of Taylor's version (Collier Books, 1963; 2 vols.) did not appear until after my book had been finished.

Longfellow to the present, have done brilliantly with one or a few; the reader must pick and choose.

2. *Anthologies, etc.*:

Goethe's Literary Essays, ed. by J. E. Spingarn. New York, 1921.
Goethe, the Story of a Man, ed. by Ludwig Lewisohn. 2 vols. New York, 1949.
Goethe's World, ed. by Berthold Biermann. New York, 1949.
Letters from Goethe, translated by M. von Herzfeld and C. A. M. Sym. New York and Edinburgh, 1957.
The Permanent Goethe, ed., selected and with an introduction by Thomas Mann. New York, 1948.
Wisdom and Experience, selections by Ludwig Curtius, translated and ed. by Hermann J. Weigand. New York, 1949.

3. *Books about Goethe; Related Works:*

Atkins, Stuart, *Goethe's Faust; A Literary Analysis.* Cambridge, [Mass.], 1958.
Bielschowsky, Albert. *The Life of Goethe.* 3 vols. Translated by William A. Cooper, New York and London, 1905-08.
Brandes, Georg. *Wolfgang Goethe.* Translated by A. W. Porterfield, 2 vols. New York, 1924.
Brown, Peter Hume. *Life of Goethe.* 2 vols. London, 1920.
Bruford, W. H. *Culture and Society in Classical Weimar, 1775–1806.* Cambridge [Eng.], 1962.
———. *Germany in the Eighteenth Century.* Cambridge [Eng.], 1935.
Butler, E. M. *The Fortunes of Faust.* Cambridge [Eng.], 1952.
Carré, J. M. *Goethe.* Trans. by Eleanor Hard. New York, 1929.
Croce, Benedetto. *Goethe.* New York, 1923.
Enright, Dennis Joseph. *Commentary on Goethe's Faust.* Norfolk, Conn., 1949.
Fairley, Barker. *Goethe's Faust.* Oxford, 1953.
———. *Goethe as Revealed in his Poetry.* Chicago, 1932.
———. *A Study of Goethe.* Oxford, 1947.

A BRIEF LIST OF WORKS IN ENGLISH

Gillies, Alexander. *Goethe's Faust; An Interpretation.* Oxford, 1957.
Jantz, Harold. *Goethe's Faust as a Renaissance Man.* Princeton, 1951.
Mann, Thomas. *Freud, Goethe, Wagner.* Translated by H. T. Lowe-Porter and R. Matthias-Reil, New York, 1937.
———. "Goethe and Tolstoy," in *Three Essays.* Translated by H. T. Lowe-Porter, New York, 1929.
Nevinson, H. W. *Goethe: Man and Poet.* London, 1931.
Palmer, P. M. and R. P. More. *The Sources of the Faust Tradition.* New York, 1936.
Peacock, Ronald. *Goethe's Major Plays.* Manchester, 1959.
Santayana, George. *Three Philosophical Poets.* Cambridge [Mass.], 1910.
Stawell, F. M. and G. Lowes Dickinson. *Goethe and Faust.* New York, 1929.
Viëtor, Karl. *Goethe, the Poet.* Translated by Moses Hadas. Cambridge [Mass.], 1949.
———. *Goethe, the Thinker.* Translated by B. Q. Morgan. Cambridge [Mass.], 1950.
Wilkinson, E. M. and L. A. Willoughby. *Goethe, Poet and Thinker.* London, 1962.

ACKNOWLEDGMENTS

I SHOULD LIKE TO THANK DIAL PRESS, NEW YORK, FOR LETTING me quote seven lines of Stawell and Dickinson's *Goethe and Faust;* Harcourt, Brace & World, New York, for permission to quote two lines from T. S. Eliot's *Collected Poems;* Harvard University Press, for allowing the use of J. M. Edmond's translation of one of Alcman's poems; Oxford University Press, New York, for allowing me to use three brief passages of Louis MacNeice's translation of *Faust;* and Mr. Ronald Peacock for permitting quotation of a passage from his *Goethe's Major Plays.*

Except as noted here, translations in this book are mine. The following translations by other hands were used, in some cases somewhat revised by me:

For *Faust*: C. F. MacIntyre (New York, n.d.) pp. 9, 52, 55; Louis MacNeice (London, n.d.) pp. 282, 295, 296; Bayard Taylor (Boston, 1871): Part I, pp. 13, 14, 32 f., 36, 66, 74, 86, 192, 208, 253, 260, 258, 298; Part II, pp. 90, 152, 215, 224, 225, 242, 261, 277 f., 229, 311, 381;

ACKNOWLEDGMENTS

Stawell and Dickinson, *Goethe and Faust* (New York, 1929), pp. 199, 202, 203.

For the lyrics: E. A. Bowring, *The Poems of Goethe* (London, 1874), p. 83. H. W. Longfellow, in *Poems of Goethe* (Boston, 1882), p. 53. J. S. Dwight, *Select Minor Poems of Goethe and Schiller* (Boston, 1839), pp. 93, 114, 115. Also R. D. Boylan, *Wilhelm Meister's Apprenticeship* (London, 1855), p. 516. Charles Des Voeux, *Torquato Tasso* (Weimar, 1833), p. 187. Anna Swanwick, *Iphigenia in Tauris* in *The Dramatic Works of Goethe* (Boston, 1884), p. 30. *Lyra Graeca*, I, 77 (the Loeb edition; London and New York, 1928) for J. M. Edmonds' translation of Alcman's poem.

INDEX

A. GENERAL

Aeschylus, 135
Alcman, 69 f.
"Anacreontic" writers, 14 f.
Aristides, 12
Aristotle, 17
Atkins, Stuart, 191, 191 n., 195
Augustine, Saint, 11

Babbitt, Irving, 2 f.
Bayle, Pierre, 15
Beethoven, Ludwig van, 1
Beutler, Ernst, 196
Bible, The, 18, 31, 110 f., 147
Bielschowsky, Albert, 139 n.
Bildungsroman, 7 f., 16 f., 52 ff., 85 f., 88–91
Boccaccio, 10
Bodmer, J. J., 16
Bourbon-Conti, Stéphanie de, 81
Boy's Magic Horn, The, 100
Brahms, Johannes, 67

Brandes, Georg, 34
Breitinger, J. J., 16
Brentano, Clemens, 1
Brion, Friederike, 21 f., 27 f., 109
Büchner, Georg, 47
Butler, Samuel, 8
Byron, George Gordon, 2, 9, 12, 135, 208 f.

Caesar, Julius, 192
Carlyle, Thomas, 8, 122
Casanova de Seingalt, G. J., 28
Cellini, Benvenuto, 12
Cervantes Saavedra, Miguel de, 6, 186
Chamisso, Adalbert von, 136
Chateaubriand, F.R. de, 41
Constant, Benjamin, 41
Corneille, Pierre, 17
Croce, Benedetto, 10

235

INDEX

Dante, 2, 106, 221
Darwin, Charles, 13
Delacroix, Eugène, 174
Dickens, Charles, 8
Diderot, Denis, 12, 17 f.
"Dies irae," 169

Eckermann, J. P., 11 f., 14, 62, 122, 177, 178, 180, 192, 209, 221
Eliot, T. S., 2, 121, 162
Emrich, Wilhelm, 217
Emerson, Ralph Waldo, 65
Erasmus, Desiderius, 2
Euripides, 55, 200

Fairley, Barker, 72, 169
Faust, Johann, 136
Fielding, Henry, 53
Firdusi, 113
Foscolo, Ugo, 41
France, Anatole, 8
Frederick II of Prussia, 15, 16
Freud, Sigmund, 38

Genesis, Book of, 154
George, Stefan, 45
Gide, André, 3, 55
Gillies, Alexander, 140, 158, 191 n.
Giorgione, 157
Goethe, August von, 79, 81
Goethe, Christiane von, see Vulpius, Christiane
Goethe, Cornelia, 20
Goethe, Elisabeth, 19, 79 (Goethe's mother)
Goethe, Johann Caspar, 19, 20
Goethe, Johann Wolfgang von
  As a scientist: 13 f., 71 f., 93, 95

Life: 1 f., 13, 19–29, 42 f., 49–52, 53 f., 70–76, 80 f., 82–84, 99 f., 108–112, 119
Works: see Index "B"
Goldsmith, Oliver, 36, 109
Gothic architecture, 24 f.
Gottsched, J. C., 16
Greco, El, 220
Gundolf, Friedrich, 22, 47

Hafiz, 113, 116
Haller, Albrecht von, 16
Hamann, Johann Georg, 23, 36
Hawthorne, Nathaniel, 13
Heffner, R.-M. S., 191 n.
Hemingway, Ernest, 41
Herder, Johann Gottfried, 17, 22–24, 25, 30 f., 36, 51, 71, 75, 78, 81, 99, 110, 113, 134
Hesse, Hermann, 3 f., 8
Hölderlin, Friedrich, 41, 208
Hofmannstahl, Hugo von, 4, 122
Homer, 17, 23, 39, 75, 96 f., 135
Hüsgen, H. S., 110
Humboldt, Wilhelm von, 178

Ibsen, Henrik, 6

Job, Book of, 135
John, Book of, 147, 164
Joseph II, Emperor, 19
Joyce, James, 3
Jung, C. G., 184 n.

Kafka, Franz, 8, 13, 41, 91, 192
Kalidasa, 135
Kant, Immanuel, 1, 23, 128
Karl August, Duke, 49, 50, 51, 52, 67, 68, 70, 79, 80, 119
Keats, John, 126, 208
Keller, Gottfried, 8

INDEX

Killy, Walther, 104
Klopstock, F. G., 2, 5, 14, 16, 20, 39
Ku-Klux Klan, 32

Laugier, Abbé Marc-Antoine, 25
Leibniz, G. W. von, 135
Lessing, Gotthold Ephraim, 15, 16, 17, 136
Levetzow, Ulrike von, 119 n.
Lichtenberg, G. C., 12
Liebestod, 34 f, 118, 198
Longfellow, Henry W., 69
Lucretius, 142
Luther, Martin, 2, 18, 31, 147

Macpherson, James, see "Ossian"
Magnus, Rudolf, 72
Mann, Thomas, 2 f., 8, 34, 41, 47, 52, 61, 85 f., 104, 119, 136, 194 n., 195, 201
Marlowe, Christopher, 136
May, Kurt, 107
Melville, Herman, 6, 12
Meredith, George, 8
Meyer, Heinrich, 122
Miller [Möller], Filippo (Goethe's pseudonym in Rome), 75
Milton, John, 15
Möser, Justus, 30
Moses, 218
Mozart, Wolfgang Amadeus, 1, 3, 56, 107, 136, 178

naparte, 99 f.

Nietzsche, Friedrich Wilhelm, 6, 11 f.
Nostradamus, 141

Novalis (Friedrich von Hardenberg), 34, 85, 91, 118

"Ossian," 17, 22, 23, 24, 36, 39
Ovid, 77, 213 n.

Palladio, Andrea, 74
Peacock, Ronald, 152, 159
Percy, Bishop Thomas, 17
Pietism, 15, 38, 57, 85
Pindar, 23
Plato, 1, 124, 127
Plutarch, 184
Politzer, Heinz, 56
Pompey, 192
Priapea, 78
Prometheus, 24 f., 28, 42, 141
Propertius, 4, 77

Rabelais, François, 60
Racine, Jean, 2, 6, 53, 57
Raphael, 72, 74, 195
Rehder, Helmut, 191 n.
Reik, Theodor, 28 n.
Richardson, Samuel, 15, 36
Riemer, F. W., 122
Rilke, Rainer Maria, 44
Rodin, Auguste, 44
Rolland, Romain, 8
Rousseau, Jean Jacques, 11, 17, 36, 38, 110, 111, 134

Sachs, Hans, 140
Santayana, George, 74, 135, 142, 148, 154, 159, 179 f., 188, 209
Sappho, 4
Schiller, Friedrich von, 1, 10, 49, 50, 51, 57, 82–84, 89, 90 f., 99, 107, 122, 128, 160, 194 n.

INDEX

Schlegel, A. W. von, 100
Schlegel brothers, 100
Schlegel, Friedrich von, 113, 135
Schönemann, Lili, 27, 28, 43
Schopenhauer, Arthur, 118
Scott, Walter, 32
Senancour, E. P. de, 41
Shakespeare, William, 1, 2, 5, 6, 17, 22, 23, 24 f., 30 f., 32, 48, 53, 85 f., 88, 111, 124, 135, 174, 175, 179 n., 217 n.
Shelley, Percy B., 208
Sophocles, 135
"Spies *Faustbook*," 136
Spinoza, Baruch, 24, 39, 46, 65, 66, 110, 134, 165, 180
Staël, Mme. A. L. G. de, 100
Staiger, Emil, 1, 44
Stein, Charlotte von, 27, 52, 53 f., 63, 65, 68, 71, 72, 76, 79, 120
Steinbach, Erwin von, 25
Stifter, Adalbert, 8
Storm and Stress, The, 28–30, 36, 38, 106, 134, 141, 147, 153 f., 174

Thomas, Calvin, 191 n., 212
Tibullus, 4, 77
Titian, 157
Twaddell, W. F., 191 n.

Valéry, Paul, 3, 136
Vergil, 55, 80
Vicq d'Azyr, Felix, 71 n.
Viëtor, Karl, 127, 137 n.
Voltaire, F. M. Arouet de, 2, 12, 15, 111, 143
Voss, J. H., 97
Vulpius, Christiane, 79, 94

Wagner, Richard, 118, 195
Wieland, Christoph Martin, 15, 16 f., 51, 52
Wilkinson, E. M., 61
Willemer, J. J., 115
Willemer, Marianne von, 27, 115, 118
Winckelmann, J. J., 11, 16, 57, 74, 98
Wolf, Friedrich August, 96
Wolff, Christian, 16
Wordsworth, William, 2

Young, Edward, 17, 23

B. GOETHE'S WORKS

"Achilleis," 97 f.
Citizen General, The, 4
Clavigo, 4, 28
Divan, West-Easterly: see "Lyrics"
Egmont, 5, 11, 45–49, 54, 92, 159, 176
Elective Affinities, The, 8 f., 101–106, 124
Entertainments of German Emigrés, 10

"Fairy Tale, The," 10, 91
Faust (as a whole): 6 f., 9, 10, 14, 91, 108, 118, 121, 131

Faust I: General References: 3, 5, 28, 29, 84, 98, 100 f., 132–136
  Individual Sections:
  "At the Fountain," 166
  "Auerbach's Cellar," 155 f.
  "Before the Gate," 145 f.

INDEX

"Cathedral," 160, 168 f.
"City Wall," 166 f.
"Dedication," 137
"Evening," 161 f.
"Forest and Cavern," 133, 160, 161, 163–165
"Garden," 162
"Gloomy Day. A Field," 174
"Gretchen tragedy," 158–169, 174–176
"Gretchen's Room," 165
"Martha's Garden," 165 f., 175
"Night [I]," 140
"Night [II]," 166 f.
"Night. Open Field," 174 f.
"Prelude in the Theatre," 135, 137 f.
"Prison," 160, 174–176
"Prologue in Heaven," 135, 137, 138–140, 151, 174, 176, 180
"Street," 158 f.
"Study [I]," 146
"Study [II]," 149–154
"Walpurgis Night," 155, 157, 160, 168, 169–173
"Walpurgis Night's Dream," 173 f.
"Witch's Kitchen," 76, 155, 156–158, 159

Faust II: General References: 7, 14, 106, 121, 133–136, 161, 177–179

Individual Sections:
Act I—179–186
Act II—187–199
Act III—199–210
Act IV—210–212
Act V—213–221
"Arcadia," 207–210
"Brightly Lighted Halls," 184 f.

"Classical Walpurgis Night," 190, 191–199
"Dark Gallery," 183 f.
"Deep Night," 215
"Great Courtyard before the Palace," 217 f.
"Helen Act"=(Act III); see also 151
"High-Arched, Narrow Gothic Room," 187 f.
"Interment," 218 f.
"Knight's Hall," 185 f.
"Laboratory," 189–191
"Masquerade," 182 f.
"Midnight," 215–217
"Mountain Ravines," 219–221
"Open Country," 213 f.
"Palace," 214 f.
"Pleasant Landscape," 179–181
"Pleasure Garden," 183
"Rocky Coves of the Aegean Sea," 195–199

"Faust: A Fragment," 137 n.
Fellow Culprits, The, 4
"For Shakespeare's Day," 24 f.
Götz von Berlichingen, 5, 24, 28–32, 46, 49, 68, 83, 174, 181
  First draft: 31
Hermann and Dorothea, 9 f., 81, 96 f.
Iphigenia in Tauris, 6, 13, 22, 54–58, 76
Italian Journey, 11, 76, 112
Lyrics
  "Alexis and Dora," 93 f.
  "Amyntas," 93 f.
  "At Midnight," 113
  "Autumnal Feeling," 45
  "Awaken, Friederike," 25

239

INDEX

"Betrothed, The," 130
"Bride of Corinth, The," 91 f.
"Chalice, The," 65
"Dedication," 64, 120, 180
Divan, West-Easterly, 4, 113–118
  "Gingko Biloba"–114 f.
  "Song and Formed Image" –117
  "Holy Longing"–4, 117 f.
"Divine, The," 65 f., 72
"Dornburg poems," 130
"Eagle and Dove," 35
"Early, vale and hills and garden," 130
"Erl King, The," 70
"Ganymede," 33, 40
"General Confession," 95 f.
"God and the Bajadere," 92 f., 107
"Harz Journey in the Winter," 67
"Ilmenau," 67 f.
"Inconstancy," 21
"Lili's Park," 43
"May Song," 26
"Metamorphosis of Plants, The," 95
"Mignon" poems, 5, 71, 87 f.
"Mohammed's Song," 32–34, 67, 112, 113
"On the Lake," 44 f.
"Pariah," 118 f.
"Permanence in Change," 95 f.
"Primal Words, Orphic," 130 f.
"Prometheus" (hymn), 34, 68
Roman Elegies, 76–78

"Song of the Spirits over the Waters," 66 f.
"Sonnets," 112
"Souvenir of vanished joy," 43
"Testament," 4, 128
"To the Moon," 64 f., 66
"To the Rising Full Moon," 130
"Trilogy of Passion," 119–121, 124, 130
  "To Werther"–119 f.
  "Elegy"–120 f.
  "Reconciliation"–121
Venetian Epigrams, 78–80
"Voyage," 45
"Wanderer's Night Songs," 68 f.
"Wanderer's Storm Song," 32
"Welcome and Departure," 26 f.
"Wild Rose," 26, 163
Maxims and Reflections, 12
Natural Daughter, The, 6, 81 f.
"Nausicaä," 75
"New Melusina, The," 28, 92
"Novella," 10, 129
"On German Architecture," 25
Pandora, 106–108, 181
"Pandora's Return," 35, 106 n.
Poetry and Truth, 10 f., 20, 50, 73, 108–112
"Prometheus" (frag. drama), 34 f.
Reynard the Fox, 10, 81
Roman Elegies: see "Lyrics."
Satyros, 35 f.
Stella, 28, 43 f.
Tasso, Torquato, 5, 6, 54, 58–63, 70, 76, 119, 120 f., 124, 144

INDEX

Theory of Colors, 72, 99
"Urfaust," 137 n., 174
Venetian Epigrams: see "Lyrics"
"Wandering Jew, The," 39
Werther, The Sorrows of Young,
  5, 7, 8, 17, 29, 36–41, 42, 43,
  53, 62, 75, 88, 101, 119, 141,
  144, 159
  Revision of 1787: 41

Wilhelm Meister's Apprenticeship, 5, 7 f., 9, 53, 66, 84–91,
  100, 101, 122–124, 221
Wilhelm Meister's Theatrical Mission, 52–54, 70
Wilhelm Meister's Wanderjahre, 9, 10, 121–129
"Winckelmann," 98
Xenia, 10, 84